Heart Shot

Heart Shot

For Hunters and Anglers Who Love the Outdoors

Kevin Yokum

Pleasant Word

Packaged by Pleasant Word, PO Box 428, Enumclaw, WA 98022. The views expressed or implied in this work do not necessarily reflect those of Pleasant Word. The author(s) is ultimately responsible for the design, content and editorial accuracy of this work.

ISBN 1-4141-0193-7
Library of Congress Catalog Card Number: 2004093167

Table of Contents

Acknowledgements

Several of the Biblical summaries in this book originated from our pastor, Ken Shiflet, who explains God's word better than anyone I've ever heard. Ken, thanks for allowing God to work in your life so that you may help others understand the Bible. I want to thank my family and friends for all their support and encouragement while working on this book. I want to especially thank my wife and children for their patience and understanding: Amy, Noah and Bailee, you are truly my foundation. God gives us many precious gifts, but family ranks at the top of my list. I can only hope that my wife and I are able to give our children as much love as our parents have given us.

Purpose

This book was designed to serve as encouragement for Christians and as a tool so that others may learn of God's wonderful works. Next
time you get a chance to enjoy God's magnificent
creation, take the time to give thanks and ask Him
how you can help others to experience eternal hope.
God has a purpose for each and every one of us; all
we have to do is make ourselves available.

Fun Facts: Elk are also known as wapiti, a name originating from the Shawnee Indians. Elk are the second largest antlered mammal in North America (moose are the largest). Average body size is 600 to 800 pounds, but bulls have been known to exceed 1,000 pounds. Average lifespan of elk is around 15 years, but one bull harvested in Arizona lived 25 years in the wild.

Chapter 1

* *

Losing Focus

As the giant raised his head, the sight I had waited my whole life for sauntered into view. The massive buck would score an easy 160 Boone and Crocket even though all I needed was 125 of that, since a bow rested in my hand. Adrenaline rocketed through my body because the biggest buck I had ever seen was walking straight toward my tree stand.

As the buck came within bow range, all I could do was stare at those magnificent antlers. The longer I stared, the more I became mesmerized by those antlers. And then it started.

It began with a little quiver in my leg, then one in my arm. The longer the buck stood at 25 yards, the faster the shakes spread. As I tried to draw, it felt as if my muscles had turned to jello. My sight pins were dancing like Mexican jumping beans as I desperately tried to suppress the severe shaking, but oh, those horns!

I had lost focus. It came as no surprise when my arrow passed harmlessly over the monstrous buck not even brushing a hair on his frame. I made a terrible mistake, and it cost me my only opportunity at a world-class whitetail.

How could I lose focus like that? I had harvested lots of deer in my hunting career including several nice bucks, but I wanted that particular buck worse than any other. I just couldn't get past the buck's gorgeous antlers. If only I could have focused on the buck's vital area instead of becoming obsessed with those antlers, oh, those fabulous antlers!

This disappointing story reminds me of a friend named George. Most folks considered George a pretty good guy, but he maintained one major flaw. George loved the women, and without a doubt, he was a first class womanizer. It wasn't as if George couldn't get the attention of attractive women, in fact his wife was absolutely gorgeous. Despite his trying to focus on other things, George obsessed over a good-looking woman's physical features. We all develop shortcomings as men, but George was involved in an extremely dangerous game.

Proverbs 7:26 tells of *many strong men that are slain by this type of behavior and points out that this path leads to hell.* Evidence of such wise counsel is found throughout the Bible, and even the Good Book's strongest men proved no match for powerful sins of the flesh. David, Solomon and Sampson destroyed their lives when they became fixated on women.

Although David could literally have picked from thousands of beautiful women in his kingdom, he became infatuated with Bathsheba. The obsession became so intense that David ended up plotting murder so he could gain access to her. Solomon, the wisest man in the Bible, and Sampson, the strongest man in the Bible, both became trapped when they succumbed to lusts of the flesh. These three fellows were real Bible heavyweights and yet they were easily toppled by lust. What happened to these mighty men of God? They lost focus just like thousands of people do today.

These three men took their eyes off Jesus. Just like the hunter who can't focus on a buck's vital area because of the antlers, these men obsessed over the beauty of women rather than concentrating on God's objectives. The Bible doesn't say that these men completely turned their backs on God by denying His existence, they just got sidetracked. And boy, did it cost them!

Lust of the flesh brings down a lot of people and this powerful sin is completely non-discriminatory. It doesn't care if you are rich or poor, wise or dumb, healthy or sick; all lust wants to do is control your life. Today's divorce rate is 50% and studies show that an even higher percentage of men and women admit being unfaithful to their spouses at some point. Is it any wonder? We are bombarded with images, TV shows, magazines, etc. which indicate that this type of behavior is okay.

Temptations of the flesh seem to be becoming more prevalent all the time, but in reality, this sin arena has been around since Biblical times. Proverbs 7:12 tells us that temptations of lust "*lieth in wait at every corner.*" If this type of sin was common in Biblical times, and has become even more widespread now, temptations of the flesh must be unbelievably addictive.

Fighting off temptations of the flesh is not a solitary incident. Lust surrounds us everyday and everyone, even pastors, will find themselves in daily battles against this sin. I bet you know several people right now who are actively committing adultery, fornication, viewing sexually explicit material or other such activities. But if these sins are so powerful, how can we overcome them?

Consistency is the key, and an excellent example comes from the bow hunting world. Expert bow hunters develop a regular routine of shooting so that each shot is identical. The correct stance, the right grip and proper follow through make each shot perfect. Doing the right thing time after time becomes the norm, and before long, the routine becomes second nature. Christians need to develop consistent habits that help them fight off daily temptations of the flesh.

When you face battles against lusts of the flesh, find a light (light bulb, sunlight, moonlight, any light will work). Use this light to refocus and remind yourself that Jesus was the light of the world. Putting Jesus first in your life serves as a shield against sin.

Another good practice is to withdraw pictures of your spouse and kids from your wallet. Most adults carry such pictures with them wherever they go. Take a good hard look at those pictures and ask yourself if a few minutes of physical pleasure is worth a lifetime of heartache.

A regular routine of Christian fellowship, daily devotions and prayer can develop people's character so they are better prepared to handle addictive temptations. Don't think you're incapable of being brought down by lustful ways and temptations, because they sure destroyed some of the most powerful men in the Bible.

The more you are able to successfully overcome temptations of the flesh by taking Godly action, the stronger you become. Success is contagious and one victory often leads to another.

When we're shook up, we become ineffective Christians and are more likely to make bad mistakes. Satan uses anger, resentment, jealousy, and all types of emotions to get us shook up.

Don't make the worst mistake of your life by losing focus on Christian values. Lusts of the flesh will seek you out, but by developing Christian routines and focusing on Jesus, you can overcome them. Consequences of sins such as adultery and fornication are devastating, so don't fool around with them. Stay focused by keeping your eye on the vital area (Jesus) and not on those alluring antlers (flesh).

Fun Facts: In the eastern United States, an adult whitetail doe establishes a home range of about one square mile. Bucks cover more territory than does because approximately one year after birth, bucks are forced to leave their mother's home range. Additional miles are piled on when bucks begin searching for females during the rut. Without hunting pressure, the average lifetime expectancy of a whitetail is about 7.5 years. Of course, deer in captivity can live for much longer because they don't have to worry about predation or expend energy for necessities like food.

....

Chapter 2

How to Find God's Direction

I t can happen to anyone, anytime, and when it happens, fear completely seizes your body. The moment a hunter realizes they're lost, an eerie sensation engulfs them, and if you think it could never happen to you, think again.

It starts with a sinking feeling deep down in your gut. Sweat breaks out on your forehead, doubt creeps into your thoughts and indecision paralyzes your movements.

Where do you turn? What do you do? Panic, the dire enemy of a hunter, takes over and reason gets pushed aside.

Men are very particular when it comes to directions. It doesn't matter if we're on a hunting trip to the Rocky Mountains or driving the family to Wal-

Mart, we demand a detailed route that is all mapped
out. Men like to be in control. Perhaps that's why
we are so afraid of getting lost.

Ben and Jerry (we called them the ice cream boys,
even though they had nothing to do with Ben and
Jerry's ice cream) were a couple of the most experienced woodsmen I have ever known. They could
outwalk a hound dog or tackle a pack of hungry
wolves without breaking a sweat. These dynamic
brothers had developed quite a reputation as first-
rate hunters, and more often than not, at least one
of them would return with a quality buck.

Ben and Jerry had trekked over three miles into
some serious "wild country" and were well into a
December muzzleloader hunt, when it happened. A
massive snowstorm hit, and it quickly blanketed the
ground with several inches of snow. Visibility was
reduced to a few feet because thick sheets of snow
were pouring from the sky. Ignoring the topographi-
cal maps they carried, Ben and Jerry trudged through
the snow in the direction they thought was right,
and soon even the maps were of no use. The un-
thinkable had happened: Ben and Jerry lost their
way.

After becoming lost, how do you find your way?
Veteran outdoorsmen know that following a stream
downhill, using a compass or a GPS unit, watching
for the moss on the northern side of trees or back-

tracking yourself in the snow are all ways which can help a hunter regain direction.

But how can we find the Lord's direction? John 14:6 tells us, *Jesus is the way (direction), the truth, and the life.* When making life's crucial decisions, we struggle to make the right choices. How can we know for certain what God wants us to do? Here are five ways to help you find God's direction.

1. Bible – What does the Bible say about your decision? Does your decision line up with scripture or does it directly violate Biblical principles? This is an easy one. If the Bible says it's wrong, then don't do it. Remember, God tells you to avoid things that can be harmful to you. Ben and Jerry had a map, but they chose to follow their own sense of direction rather than relying on a written map. We do the same thing when we ignore God's map (Bible) and make decisions on our own.

2. Revelation of the Heart - Better known as your conscience. God gives us that little inside voice which tells us what direction to take.

3. People – God provides us with friends, church members, pastors, and others to advise us on important matters. Make sure to choose your friends carefully, and don't hesitate to call upon them for advice.

4. Wisdom – God gave humans common sense and the ability to reason.
   You sure wouldn't know it by some of the decisions we make, but deep inside each of us is a Godly wisdom. Our wisdom grows through the process of making proper decisions.

5. Open Doors – Ever pray about a difficult decision and suddenly all the obstacles were magically removed? It seems like a bulldozer plows right through one side of the problem, clearing the way for a rock solid decision. Don't underestimate the power of prayer, because it is a mighty tool.

None of these steps will magically reveal God's direction every time. Perhaps even a combination of steps may be required to find out what God wants you to do.

Whether playing video games, hunting, sports, etc., confidence is garnered by success, and finding God's direction is no different. The more we seek God's advice, follow it and experience His rewards, the greater our confidence and trust grows. Confidence and trust build relationships and there is definitely a correlation between our relationship with God and the clarity of His direction.

One of the best ways to learn about trusting God is to spend time with Him. This can be in the form of praying, reading the Bible or attending church. Ultimately, the confidence/trust factor will help us to effectively find God's direction. In Jeremiah 10:23 God reminds us that we don't have the ability to make correct decisions on our own. However, if we follow God's guidance and seek His direction, we can be right every time.

God doesn't want a half-hearted effort or indecision from any part of our lives, He wants total commitment. The more confidence we have in something, the easier it is to commit. Ben and Jerry were so disoriented and indecisive that they didn't have the confidence to decide on which direction to go. They couldn't make a commitment. Do you have the confidence to make an honest commitment to God today? It's not too late. Start applying the five directive steps to your decision-making and watch your confidence grow. You've got nothing to lose except lots of bad decisions.

What a thrill it is to get a clear direction from God after struggling with a tough decision. Clear directions provide much needed assurance, and if direction comes from God, you can be positive that it is the way to go.

Fun Facts: Elk are deceivingly fast. They can reach 35 to 40 mph when running short distances, and over long distances, elk can sustain speeds up to 28 mph. Elk are good swimmers and excellent jumpers. Jumping eight foot high fences is no problem and in some documented cases, elk have cleared ten foot fences. Most ranch fences are no higher than five feet, but elk have a bad habit of striking the top of the obstacle they are leaping over. Ranchers can testify that when 200 elk jump a cattle fence, a repair job is usually necessary.

Chapter 3

The Crushing Blow

I t's funny that through all of life's achievements, it is the disappointments of life that we seem to remember the most.

Sometimes I wake up in the middle of the night reliving the "big game," which of course, we lost in the final minutes. I recall, in vivid detail, a particular contest that I should have won but didn't, and oh yes, I have replayed over and over the Montana hunt where I missed that magnificent elk. Many times, I speculate that if I had only acted differently, the outcome would have been better.

It's a real thrill to harvest a big game animal and I have been fortunate to bag my share, including some really nice bucks and bull elk. However, the failure of one particular elk hunting encounter still brings to mind the bitter disappointment I felt on that November hunt.

Elk hunting in Montana is always special, but this hunt was really important to me because I figured it would probably be my last for quite some time. My family wasn't poor, but we weren't in an economic bracket that would allow us to hunt elk in Montana each year either. The bottom line was that I had to make the most of my opportunity and for me that meant putting down a big bull.

We were hunting the third week of Montana's fall rifle season, which can be one of the toughest times to harvest elk, especially if weather conditions are mild. It was late in the afternoon on day four of a six day hunt, and I was watching a high elevation "park," (open fields or grazing land where elk come to feed). The guide had taken another hunter to watch a nearby park, so I ended up basically by myself. About an hour before dark, elk started to move into the open, and it wasn't long until some nice bulls appeared, but they were well out of range. Well, I waited for what seemed an eternity for the elk to move into shooting range as darkness quickly closed in. Half frozen, but yet quivering with anticipation, I lay down on the ground and waited for the biggest bull to move into the open for a clear shot. When the big 5x5 stopped in my scope's cross hairs,

I pulled the trigger. Boom! Nothing happened. I shot again, Boom! The bull never moved. I fired again, and this time the elk had heard enough commotion and ran back into the timber.

The guide and his other hunter joined me as we went to look for blood. Earlier I told the guide that I had killed whitetail deer at 500 yards and could fire a lethal shot up to that distance. Well, as we stepped off the distance, I soon realized my mistake. Counting a little over 600 yards to the spot the bull had stood, I knew the only chance my bullets had of hitting that elk were to have ricochet off a flat rock some 100 yards away.

I was devastated. With only two more days remaining in the hunt and opportunities in very short supply, I knew I had blown my chance for a nice bull. To make matters worse, unknown to me, the elk had been headed right for the other hunter who could have gotten a good shot at the bulls.

It was a long ride back to camp with the three of us jammed in the front of our guide's pickup truck. I dreaded to go to dinner, because every night at the dinner table, members of the hunting party chatted about events of the day. With weather conditions so mild, every opportunity at bull elk were precious so I knew everyone around the table would be talking about the young kid's (me) screw up.

As my family members and hunting companions ribbed me about my missed opportunity, I was
miserable, but I managed to take their comments in
good nature. How easy it would have been to scream
at them and slam the door on my way out. Many
times we express ourselves by misguiding our anger and sometimes God becomes the primary target. Has something ever happened in your life that
made you angry with God?

Well, join the crowd. You know we're not alone
at venting our frustration on almighty God. In fact,
several of the most noted men in the Bible became
angry at God when certain events occurred in their
lives. John the Baptist, whom Jesus said among men
were none better, was offended by God, and wondered why he been imprisoned. Even David, the
mighty king, became enraged at God when his friend
was killed while attempting to do what he thought
was helpful. God is all-powerful, and I sure am glad
that He doesn't mistake the moment for the man
(judge us by our actions when we misdirect our
anger).

When we get frustrated, like I was during my
elk hunt, we often react by doing stupid things.
Anger towards God can cause us to stop giving Him
our time or money. At other times it's not uncom-
mon to see folks stop attending church after becoming angry at God. Sometimes, we give up on God

altogether and return to our own methods of living. How silly it seems to think that we're getting even with God by not obeying Him, when in reality all we're doing is hurting ourselves.

How to Deal with Disappointment

1) **Refocus on the past**
Look back to the times when God has comforted and helped you in the past. Have confidence that He will do it again. God promises in Heb. 13:5 that *He will never leave nor forsake us*. God is mighty, and He loves you no matter what you have done. That night in Montana, recalling past hunting experiences helped boost my confidence and God helped me realize that success would revisit me again. Refreshed that God was by my side, I knew that dwelling on that day's failure would be a waste of time.

2) **Look at where you are now**
Confirm your present situation. That night in Montana I realized, Wow! I still have two more days to hunt elk in Montana. Are you where God wants you to be in your life? Is there some hidden sin that is causing or contributing to your disappointment? Ask God for guidance so that you can get where He wants you because let's face it, God knows best.

3) **Put God in the middle of the problem**
   During dreaded dinner chastisement, God
   helped me to sustain my temper. Instead of
   acting foolishly, He helped me to laugh along
   with my companions and to share in the fellowship of the evening. Laughing along with
   my companion's good-natured kidding was
   much better than sulking around, and believe me, I felt like crawling under the table.
   If you're in the middle of a problem, ask God
   for help. Through prayer, you can talk directly to God, and He doesn't have call waiting. Put God in the middle of your next problem and watch what happens.

4) **Look to the future**
   Take comfort in knowing that your whole
   life is ahead of you and God has great things
   in store. That night in Montana as I lay in
   my bed sorely disappointed, God showed me
   that although I had placed heavy emphasis
   on harvesting an elk, things weren't so bad.
   He helped me realize that many more successful hunts lay ahead and perhaps I would
   appreciate them even more because of this
   missed elk.

Christian or not, all of us will have to deal with
big disappointments in our lives. Having God to help
us deal with disappointments is a huge help. It sad-
dens me to see some of my non-Christian friends

struggle with problems without the aid of the Great Comforter (Jesus). If you're having a difficult time right now, ask Jesus for comfort and invite Him into your life. I guarantee that it will be the best decision you ever make. If you're a Christian and have back-slidden, then turn your troubles over to Jesus. God tells us in Mal. 3:7, *"Ye are gone away from mine ordinances; and have not kept them. Return unto me and I will return unto you."* Get back into the hunt and never, ever give up.

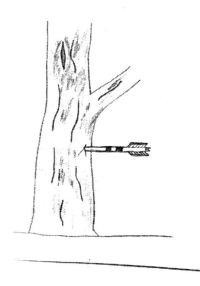

Fun Facts: What does it take to get a whitetail buck in the record book? Bow kills are recorded in Pope and Young by measuring inches of antler. The minimum Pope and Young score for typical racks is 125 and 155 for non-typicals. Boone and Crockett records firearm kills in a similar fashion. Minimum score for the all-time Boone and Crockett record book is 170 for typical racks and 195 for non-typicals. Boone and Crockett also recognizes the minimum score of 160 typical and 185 non-typical in a separate award book which is updated every three years.

....

Chapter 4

Outrageous Gifts

Trying to catch my breath after sprinting across the lawn, I cautiously pulled open the door. Sweet joy over Calvary, it was here! Like many outdoors enthusiasts, I rush to the mailbox each December afternoon, not to find Christmas cards, but to look for Christmas editions of Cabelas and L.L. Bean catalogs. Wives please take note, do not throw away any Cabela's catalogs without first checking with your husbands (arguments and even a few domestic incidents have resulted from such oversights).

Traditionally, my family has always celebrated the birth of Christ with dinners, reading the Christmas story, and oh yes, plenty of gifts. Through the years, I have received some awesome Christmas gifts: guns, my first bow, a motorcycle and numerous other hunting and fishing related items. I used to get so excited the night before Christmas that I would be unable to sleep, although I pretended to just in case Santa was checking.

One gift I will never forget was a plane ticket to Montana for a combination elk and deer hunt. My father and I, along with a friend, had hunted elk in Montana the previous year and experienced an incredible adventure. Due to economic considerations, it was doubtful that we would be able to return to Montana for some time. However, Mom came to the rescue, making the necessary sacrifices so her husband and son could return for another dream hunt.

My dad and I were so excited about the tickets Mom purchased that we couldn't keep quiet. We immediately called our friend and found out that he also got a ticket from his wife. Excitement and shenanigans ran rampant as we danced around the Christmas tree with visions of monster elk running through our scopes. Those hunts in Montana were some of the best times I have ever experienced, and stories from those hunts still frequent our conversations.

Christmas is all about giving, and for years my wife and I desired to give both of our parents something special. Through the years, they have given us so much and continue to do so even now. We struggled with our goal of finding unique gifts that each of our parents would really enjoy, but would never purchase on their own.

I had the pleasure of taking my father-in-law on a trout fishing trip to Yellowstone National Park for some of the finest fly fishing in the world. It was his first trip out west and his first journey on a plane. Just before Christmas, we were celebrating my son's birthday when my mother-in-law revealed that she would love to see Billy Joel and Elton John in concert. Of course, the closest concert had been sold out for months, but we managed to secure tickets, although they were a bit higher than regular price. The gift package was completed when we sent my parents on a scenic trip to Montana where they experienced the majesty of Yellowstone and the Rocky Mountains.

The cost of each trip was worth every penny, even though material gifts can never repay all the priceless love our parents have given us. All trips resulted in joyous adventures that none of our families will ever forget.

Speaking of outrageous gifts, how about the gift God gave to all of us? God sent his only son, Jesus, to die on the cross at Calvary so that we could obtain the gift of eternal life (John 3:16). Talk about a high price to pay for a gift! Not even *EBay* carries that kind of gift.

Being the father of two children, it wasn't until I became a dad and felt the magic bond between father and children, that I could really appreciate the magnitude of God's gift. The Bible makes no bones about it, either we spend eternity in a wonderful place called heaven or a tormented existence burning in hell. Without the special gift of Jesus dying on the cross, we would not be able to enter heaven.

The Christmas present giving tradition began when the wise men brought gifts to baby Jesus. During the hustle and bustle of the Christmas season, which is really about the birth of Jesus, I wonder if we ever think about what Jesus would like for Christmas.

Let's examine the gifts that the wise men brought to Jesus. These gifts were very strange gifts for an infant. The wise men brought Jesus gold (money), frankincense (perfume), and myrrh (embalming fluid).

The gifts portray a picture of what Jesus wants for Christmas. The gold represented money or the very best that people could give in Biblical times. Right now, Jesus wants us to give our very best to Him. He wants 100% access to our lives just like we would give to someone we share a close relationship with.

Frankincense was a type of perfume or incense used in worship services, and was considered to be one of the finest commercial scents in Biblical times. People used frankincense during a really special worship service to honor God. Jesus was trying to show us that He wants our worship, not just on Sunday mornings, but in all aspects of our lives. Let's face it, if we followed Jesus' direction, our lives would run much smoother.

Myrrh, or embalming fluid, is the oddest of the three gifts. Myrrh was used in the same fashion as modern day embalming fluid. It was placed on the bodies of the dead to keep them from smelling. This gift was a reminder that through Jesus there is life after death. We are preserved in His grace, but we must take action on our part to receive everlasting life. Jesus has provided the gift of eternal life for those willing to accept Him as Savior, and He has made it so easy that anyone, anywhere can do it. Romans 10:13 tells us, "*Whosoever shall call upon the name of the Lord shall be saved.*" This will be the most important decision you will ever make.

Our pastor often says that many people will miss heaven by 18 inches (distance from head to heart). People try to make salvation too complicated, but salvation is simple. The truth of the matter is that Jesus paid the price for our sins on the cross and the only way for each of us to obtain eternal life is by accepting Him into our heart.

Looking for the perfect gift this season? Take a look at Jesus' Christmas list. If you haven't accepted Jesus in your life, then that's what He wants. Jesus promises that if you accept Him, give 100% effort and worship Him, He will bless you. Blessings can come in all forms, but rest assured with God in your life, you will be happier than ever imagined. The Bible is filled with examples of Jesus' blessings, and people who followed God's instructions were rewarded with bountiful gifts. As you plan your shopping this holiday season, don't forget about the most astonishing gift of all, Jesus.

Fun Facts: The deer breeding season is commonly called the rut. The rut lasts for a few weeks each fall and is primarily triggered by hormone production. Female deer come into estrus cycle for 24 to 48 hours so a buck must pick up the estrus scent trail, find that doe and breed her in that brief period for successful conception to take place. If a doe is not bred during that cycle, she comes back into a second estrus cycle about 28 days later. This later period is referred to as the secondary rut. Buck activity during the rut reaches a yearly high as you might expect.

• •

Chapter 5

What to Do When Everything Goes Wrong

J ust when you think that things can't get any worse, they do. Problems seem to come in waves and one ordeal seems to lead to others. To make matters worse, problems typically arise at the most inopportune times.

On a recent bow hunt, I experienced one such atrocious day. The rut was just starting to reach its peak and for a bow hunter, the peak of the rut is the most exciting time to be in the woods. Adding to my excitement, the moon phase calendar, if you believe in that sort of thing, predicted that this particular day would be one of the season's best for buck activity. Boy was I fired up!

Things started to go haywire from the get-go. Slipping on my hunting clothes at 5:00 A.M, I acci-

41

dentally knocked a tin can off our dresser. Of course, the can was full of spare change which made a rather loud commotion, waking up my infant daughter. Most hunters know that waking up a sleepy wife in the early A.M hours is not conducive to maintaining a happy marriage. Introduce a screaming infant into the fracas, and you have quite a predicament. I ducked out of my house like a sprinting jackrabbit, muttering apologies as I retreated to the safety of my truck.

Anxious to begin the day's hunt, the first thing I did was step out of the truck right into the middle of a deep puddle. My heart deflated as I felt the instant wetness that meant my boot had just filled with water. Considering the temperature was 20 degrees, the wet boot would have quite a chilling effect on this hunt.

My foot was momentarily forgotten as I found a fresh scrape under the tree where I planned to hang my stand. Quietly, I slipped my climbing stand around the tree and started skyward. Like most hunters, I believe that silently settling into your stand under the cover of darkness greatly contributes to early morning hunting success. My stealthy efforts, however, were rewarded with a loud clang as my bow clamored against the stand. The commotion made enough noise to alert any buck within a half mile.

If the clamoring wasn't bad enough, as I was adjusting my toboggan about five minutes before daybreak, my bow release slipped from my arm and fell 20 feet to the ground. I had no choice but to climb to the ground, retrieve my release and then climb back up the tree. This was not the way I wanted to spend those initial minutes of precious morning daylight.

By now you might guess that I was pretty upset, but my troubles weren't over. About an hour after daybreak, the wind suddenly shifted so that it was blowing right over the trail leading to the fresh scrape. Any buck traveling this worn path would surely smell my scent before getting within bow range.

Like so many times before, just when you think nothing good is going to happen, a buck appears. The four-point came right down the hot trail toward the scrape almost like I had scripted the scene. Miraculously, the buck didn't pick up my scent, and as he approached the 25-yard mark, I started to draw my bow. Unexpectedly, the arrow fell off my bow rest, making a loud clink which caused the buck to spook back into the thicket.

Of course, I calmly assured myself that all was okay, and wished myself better luck next time. Yeah, right! I responded like many of us when we get angry, and I let go with some language that would have startled a street thug. Then I kicked the tree (which also helped to warm up my frozen foot), and was in the process of banging my head against the tree trunk when I spotted movement. Unbelievably, that darn four-point had circled and was coming right back toward my stand. The buck approached from a different direction offering an even better shooting opportunity than the previous scenario. Readying my bow, I couldn't believe the buck provided me with a second chance. Forty yards, thirty, twenty, ten, holy cow, the buck stopped right under my stand! I released the arrow and watched it wiz over the top of the buck's back, barely even touching his hair. This time, the buck bolted never to return again.

I blinked at the fleeing buck, unwilling to believe what had just happened. Denial and shaken confidence forced me to look for an excuse, but I couldn't find anything to blame. How could I continue to hunt after everything had gone so wrong, and did I even want to?

At times like these I am reminded of Joseph's ordeal in the Bible. Talk about a situation where everything went wrong. Joseph started out as the favorite son of a very wealthy family, and had access to pretty much all the material things a man could want. However, his life soon turned upside down. Joseph got sold into slavery by his own brothers and was taken to a strange, foreign land. But God was with him and saw to it that Joseph ended up working for Potiphar, an important Egyptian. Sounds like a happy ending, but Joseph's saga was just getting started. Potiphar's wife falsely accused Joseph of rape because he refused to commit adultery with her. Joseph was thrown into prison without hope of release. All said and done, Joseph went through suffering for about 20 years, and he didn't deserve any of it.

What would you do in Joseph's position? Would you have become better (become stronger in your faith) or bitter (angry at God and given up)?

1) **Don't demand why**
   God has a plan for our lives, but things will occur which we won't understand. It's normal to ask God why, and it is very wise to seek guidance from Him. However, there's no point in dwelling on the question. I'm sure there were many times when Joseph asked God why bad things were happening to him, but he trusted in God and didn't dwell on his misfortune.

2) **Don't quit or become bitter**
   Twenty years of excruciating struggles is a long time to undergo torment. I don't think I could have withstood the tribulation that Joseph endured, but God knows exactly how much stress each of us can take, and He

promises never to burden us with more than
we can handle. In 1 Cor. 10:13, God tells us,
He is faithful and will not suffer you tempta-
tion above that ye are able to bear; and will
help you escape temptation that ye may be able
to bear it.

It is easy to get discouraged, but in your Christian life, you must push forward. Go to church, read
your Bible, talk to Christian friends, visit a pastor;
do whatever it takes to stay in the faith. You limit
God's ability to work in your life when you shut
him out.

About two hours after the series of embarrass-
ing debacles occurred on the previously mentioned
bow hunt, a big seven-point walked right down the
trail toward my stand. This time as I released my
arrow, I watched it strike the buck's vital area. If I
had harvested the smaller buck earlier in the day, I
never would have seen this beautiful seven-point.
Overcoming significant adversity made this seven-
point a special trophy.

Sometimes, God does things that don't make
sense to us. However, we must trust God and know
that He is sovereign. *God will not allow anything to*
happen that He can't use for his purpose (Rom. 8:28).

Like my hunting trip, Joseph's story also had a
happy ending. He continued to trust God and be-

came a stronger Christian because of the trials he endured. Many positive things came out of Joseph's struggles, but I am sure it wasn't easy. In the end, we see that Joseph became one of the most prominent men of the Bible, and he did so by staying in touch with God.

You may not immediately see the results of your perseverance like I did on that November bow hunt, but your life will be enriched if you stay in touch with God.

God sometimes uses difficulties to make us stronger, and through experience we know that troubles often force us to refocus our attention on God. When difficult times arise, will you become better or bitter? God clearly tells us in Eph. 4:31 *to put away all bitterness, wrath, anger, clamor and evil speaking.*

Remember, when everything starts to go wrong, God holds the answers. Try not to dwell on the question of why, and whatever you do, don't quit or become bitter. Whatever it takes, stay in the hunt.

Fun Facts: Bucks need three ingredients to reach trophy status: age, nutrition and genetics. In some states, 1.5 year old bucks make up 70 percent of the annual harvest. Whitetail bucks develop their premium set of antlers at age four or five. Nutrition varies with annual mast production, but best antler development occurs where high-nutrient agricultural crops are consistently available.

Chapter 6

Never Too Late

For my family, deer season is an epic event. No holiday brings our family together like Thanksgiving, which in West Virginia happens to coincide with the first week of bucks only firearm season. Even family members that we see just once a year, assemble for this time-honored occasion.

Each night all members of the family, even those not hunting during the day, gather at my Grandma's house for dinner. What a feast! The end of each exhausting day finds all the hungry hunters eagerly looking forward to a delicious evening meal. In earlier times, the instant our food was placed on the table, it became "grab, grunt and growl" as hungry hunters clawed at the food with reckless abandon. But that was then, and this is now.

The reason for the change is astounding. My grandfather, Pappa Yokum, discovered Jesus a few years and now everyone, and I mean everyone, waits until grace is offered before dinner begins. In reverence of Pappa, not a morsel is touched until grace is finished, and then of course, the grabbing and growling commences.

I recall the first time my grandfather announced that we were going to say grace before the evening meal. Everyone was shocked when the declaration was delivered and literally mouths fell open all through the house. Then, one by one, everyone closed their eyes and bowed their heads. It was a major turning point for our family.

My grandfather had shunned God for years, and few would have ever given him any hope of finding the Lord. You see, Pappa was very set in his ways like many grandparents, and he had a well deserved reputation for being a bit cantankerous at times. Not the kind of person you would put high upon your potential witness list, but Mark 10:27 tells us, "*With God all things are possible.*"

In reality, it is difficult for older folks to find God without some type of catastrophic event causing a major change in their lives. Studies show that if we don't discover God by our 20s, then it's unlikely that we ever will. When my grandfather accepted Jesus while in his 60s, it was completely unexpected. I am so proud of him for making what he calls the best decision of his life.

Pappa was a good person and a really nice man even before he got saved, but even those traits wouldn't have earned him a ticket to heaven. Only by accepting Jesus as his Savior was my grandfather able to write his name in the book of life.

Pappa's changed life has affected others in our family who look to him for guidance. After he got saved, some were confused by the change in Pappa, but there was no mistaking the joy which radiated from him like never before. Now our deer season gatherings resound with a new energy. The example set by Pappa has established renewed reverence for our Heavenly Father, and this example has rubbed off on some family members.

How reassuring to know that it is never too late to accept Jesus. Jesus paid the price on the cross and we can get to heaven by simply asking Him to be our Savior. There's no timetable for accepting Jesus, and He is available anywhere, anytime. Some accept Jesus on their deathbed as senior citizens while others make the commitment early in life, but you must be careful. We never know when our earthly life may end. Proverbs 27:1 says, "*Boast not thyself of tomorrow; for thou knowest not what a day may bring forth.*" Don't put off the most important decision of your life until tomorrow, because you have no guarantee that tomorrow will ever arrive. Do it now!

Waiting to make that life-altering decision is a tremendous gamble. Satan loves the waiting game, and all too often, he uses it as a manipulating tool. Satan knows that he can't convince people that God isn't real, so he tries to confuse us so that we put off making that life saving decision. For many, tomorrow never arrives. Either they keep putting the decision off indefinitely, or their lives end before they commit.

My Pappa is so embarrassed about taking so long to find God. He realizes that so much time was wasted in which he could have been serving the Lord. Life is so much more enriched when God is guiding your life. Pappa is lucky. He made the vital decision to accept Christ while he still had time. What a powerful testimony he offers today!

Unworthy of God's attention? Hey, join the crowd. We're all unworthy, but God loves us anyway. In fact, God loves us no matter who we are or what we have done, and He can use anyone to glorify His kingdom. Look at the apostle Paul who wrote most of the New Testament. Did you know that before he found God, he was an evil king named Saul who hated God? He actually hunted down Christians, killing and torturing them. Not exactly the resume that we would expect the most prolific writer of the New Testament to maintain, but when God takes charge, wonderful things happen.

God cares more about the present than he does about your past, and remember, it's never too late to accept God. Inviting God into your life is like becoming the Cinderella team in the NCAA basketball finals when the momentum has just shifted in your direction. You feel a huge burden lifted from your shoulders and that nothing can stop you. The awesome truth is with God's help nothing can stop you.

Next hunting season, as you prepare to "chow down" with your hunting buddies, take time to give God thanks. And remember, it's never too late to experience God's greatness.

Fun Facts: Chronic Wasting Disease (CWD) is a neurological disease found in deer and elk. Known by bacteriologists as spongiform encephalopathies, CWD attacks the brains of infected deer or elk resulting in death of the animal. The publicity of mad cow disease has alerted hunters across the country to CWD and currently the disease has been restricted to twelve states and two Canadian provinces. While CWD is similar to mad cow disease there's no known relationship between CWD and humans.

Chapter 7

Study the Map

Ben's trophy room was incredible. No matter
what or where he hunted, Ben always seemed
to experience success. Although his trophy
room is breathtaking, it wasn't until Ben came home
with a giant 6x6 bull from his first western elk hunt
that it became blatantly obvious that he was employing some kind of specialized hunting strategy.
No one understood how Ben, who had never been
elk hunting, could be so successful on his first try.
Beginner's luck, someone said, and I believed it. But
when Ben took trips to Canada, Ohio, Kansas and
Pennsylvania, he came home just as successful.

Ben doesn't have a lot of money to hire guides
and he doesn't hunt on private preserves, so every
successful hunt has to be attributed to his hunting

ability. Basically, Ben does all the work on his own. Many of his hunting buddies continued to be amazed by Ben's hunting accomplishments, so one day we cornered him, and under the threat of bodily harm, forced Ben to reveal his secret.

"Boys," he said, "It's simple. Before going on a trip, I spend time studying maps of prospective hunting areas looking for natural funnels and travel corridors between food sources and bedding zones. I pay special attention to the area's food sources and study local weather patterns so that I know what to expect on these hunts. If you want to upgrade your hunting success, study the map," stated Ben.

Well, I wasn't convinced. I figured Ben was holding out on us. But when our friend Joe, who was basically a bumbling klutz in the woods, started harvesting big whitetails, turkey and even an elk, I started to wonder. "Try the map thing, you idiot!" Joe barked at me. After recapping Joe's recent hunting success, I could no longer doubt that there was something special about the map strategy.

Sounds like the Christian life, doesn't it? When people see happiness radiating from Christians, no matter how hard they try to ignore it, eventually they acknowledge that there's something special about the Christian way.

Taking Joe's advice, I started studying a map before going on hunts, and it has turned into one of my most successful hunting tools. Studying maps helps me understand what to expect on my hunts and I see more game than ever before. When we listen to wise instruction, good things happen.

This tale reminds me of a sermon our pastor recently gave on the three wise men. I never thought much about the wise men other than their traditional role in the Christmas story. But did you know they were three of only a few people who really prepared for the birth of Christ? They even knew when the Christ child, Jesus, was to be born. Herod didn't know. Bible scholars and preachers didn't know. Even the shepherds weren't aware of the happenings until the angels appeared unto them.

But, how did the wise men know? Were they that smart? No, if they were so smart, they would have seen right through Herod's wicked scheme to kill Jesus. God had to instruct the wise men not to return to Herod once they found baby Jesus. The wise men knew about Jesus because they studied their map, the Bible!

At this point in history, only portions of the modern day Bible had been written. However, Micah and Daniel were two of those Biblical books, and both give an account of Jesus' glorious birth. These portions of the Bible also tell where Jesus was to be born and provide details of His birth.

The wise men had studied and researched their map. They knew the scriptures well enough to figure out when one of the most important events in history would occur. The Bible didn't give the exact date of Jesus' birth, but it did give a "ballpark" figure so that the wise men figured out approximately when the birth would take place.

But where were all the other astute people? Wouldn't you think that with all the "holy" people about, some would have studied the scriptures enough to know of Jesus' birth? People back in Biblical times were probably just like many folks today in that they acknowledge a God, but they don't take Him seriously or study His word like they should.

But the wise men took God seriously. They were so sure about the directions from the map (Bible) that they traveled a tremendous distance to Bethlehem to participate in the extraordinary birth. God didn't let them down either. Once the wise men began their journey, God gave them a brilliant star to follow. Imagine the excitement when that star appeared and the wise men realized that all their studies had paid off. What an incredible feeling it must have been to know they were going to see the King. When we take the initiative to live according to God's plan, the Lord enriches our lives way more than we deserve.

Once the wise men saw baby Jesus in the manager, they fell to their knees and worshipped Him. This was no simple affair, because to bow down before anyone other than a king was virtually a death sentence. So the three wise men literally staked their lives on the belief that this baby, laying in the midst of smelly farm animals, was the King of the world. The wise men weren't worried because their studies revealed without a shadow of a doubt that the baby was Jesus. What confidence in the Lord's word these men exhibited!

When Jesus comes to earth a second time, He won't be a baby. He will return as Judge of the world. Will you be ready for Him? Will you know when He is coming?

In Matt. 24:44, the Bible is clear that *no man knows the exact hour when our Savior will return*, but God does give us signs in the Bible that provide a timeline for the Lord's return. Matthew 24 reveals many of these signs, and I have to be honest with you, all the signs indicate that the time is near. Don't take my word for it, study the map. It will not only make you a better hunter: It will make your life better than you ever dreamed.

Fun Facts: A survey conducted by western guides revealed that over half of successful elk hunters had taken their animals with .30–06, .270 or similar calibers. An estimated 75 percent of the harvested animals were taken at less than 200 yards. In a multi-state survey, western guides indicated that the number one misconception of hunters was that they must be able to shoot long distances to harvest elk. Almost unanimously, guides placed a much higher priority on hunters being comfortable with their rifles than they did on long distance shooting ability.

....

Chapter 8

.270 or .30–06?

The carotid artery in my neck nearly exploded. Blood poured through my vessels and I sensed heat rushing throughout my body. Blood-red face, accelerated breathing and bulging eyeballs indicated that my temper was about to burst wide open. Serious damage can occur when our brain forgets to engage before our mouth starts moving and an argument provides a great avenue for this to occur. The resulting rage an argument generates can create emotional injuries and scars that last a lifetime.

As a group of family friends were preparing to go elk hunting in Colorado, an interesting scenario developed. The group's most boisterous member, Jim, just purchased a brand new Swarovski scope for his .270, and he was boasting that his rifle would outperform anyone's 30–06.

Jim was an expert marksman and he wasn't shy about proclaiming his shooting ability. Jim prided himself on his long range shooting, and make no mistake about it, the man was an accurate shooter.

One afternoon all of the westward hunters gathered on the range to make sure their rifles were in peak condition. Jim brought his new .270 outfit and was determined to demonstrate its capabilities. Well, certain members of the party decided to play a little joke on Jim. After firing each shot Jim always went down range to examine his target. While he was gone, someone would move his scope adjustment a couple of clicks to alter his shot placement. Not used to missing his target, it didn't take many misses before Jim became very agitated. Predictably, all of Jim's buddies were pouring on comments about their dependable .30–06s and how they never had any reliability problems.

Jim couldn't understand what was happening with his new rifle and expressed his frustration by yelling at his friends. Pride had overcome him, and he couldn't handle the strain. The situation became so explosive that everyone became too afraid to tell Jim what really happened.

Some of the most bitter fights I have ever seen started with two people arguing about trivial matters. I have literally seen friendships torn apart over disagreements about which rifle is better, the .270 or .30–06. You have probably seen them too: Arguments that begin over whether a 150 or 180 grain bullet flies straighter or whether a bolt action rifle shoots more accurately than an automatic.

These topics make great debates, but many times disagreements escalate into full blown arguments which end up causing hard feelings or worse. People stop talking to each other, good friends become enemies or family turmoil can be stirred up. Families are particularly vulnerable to arguments because of the frequent interaction among members. In worst case scenarios, physical altercations can be the end result.

And for what? When is the last time you saw anyone win an argument? No one wins when people argue. Even when bested by an adversary, we are usually too stubborn to admit defeat.

Let's revisit the .270/.30–06 issue. Growing up in deer country, it seemed that everyone had an old reliable .30–06 semi-automatic rifle. Problems started when the new generation of .270 hunters invaded the home territory of all those dedicated .30–06 sportsmen and years of turmoil ensued.

In reality, there is little difference between the two calibers. Both are effective deer rifles with similar ballistics and many of the same characteristics.

Getting into serious arguments over trivial differences is pretty silly if you stop and think about it, but when pride gets in the way, trouble usually follows.

The Bible addresses any problem that we may encounter on this earth and arguing is certainly covered. In Romans 14:1, *God tells us to avoid arguments altogether*. Sounds simple, but our pride loves to barge into the middle of passive debates and transform them into heated arguments.

God also tells us that it is okay to have different opinions on topics, as long as the Bible doesn't say that it is wrong. Heck, if everyone had the same interests or agreed all the time, the world would be a boring place. God tells us that things like murder or adultery are wrong (Ten Commandments), but He doesn't specify whether a .270 or .30–06 is the best deer rifle, so the debate will probably continue.

God clearly tells us in the Bible that there is only one way to enter heaven, and that is by accepting His Son, Jesus Christ. Some folks will try to argue that all good people will go to heaven, but there is no debate on this subject. The Bible tells us that salvation through Jesus is the only way to end up in heaven. *"No man cometh unto the Father, but by me"* (John 14:6).

Hints for handling arguments

1. Part of our Christian lifestyle is simply not to enter into harsh arguments. *"A soft answer turnth away wrath, but grievous words stir up anger"* (Prov. 15:1). Remember, no one wins an argument. Walking away from an argument is real easy to talk about, but when your "know-it-all" brother-in-law prods you with comments about your little "bean shooter" .270, the situation may require restraint.

2. Read your Bible. The Bible is full of stuff on how to handle debates and avoid arguments, and it is particularly helpful in offering advice on how to control your temper. God's book is also filled with examples of people who avoided arguments and those that encountered problems when they didn't.

3. Know that it is God's desire for us to avoid arguments. If you examine the big picture, you can see that arguing over deer rifles has little significance in the grand scheme of life, and it's not worth the possible consequences of a contentious argument.

4. Satan loves for us to argue. Arguing opens up avenues for him to conduct his work. Satan is a master at using pride to make arguments escalate out of control. Make no mistake, Satan will find the most destructive aspect of an argument and use it to cause problems. Pride, grudges and selfishness are

all used to impact emotions and Satan can really use our temper to interfere with God's plan for our lives.

Hunters love to disagree and there is nothing wrong with a lively debate. But be careful that your next debate doesn't rage into a serious argument. Debates over trivial matters are not worth the price of a serious argument, even if you're right and your brother-in-law is wrong.

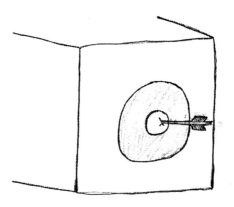

Fun Facts: Hunters love to estimate age on live deer by observing physical characteristics such as antler development, hair coloration or body size. Body size is the most accurate of these subjective aging methods because mature bucks often develop a deep chest cavity that gives a bulky appearance to the deer's body. However, the only proven way to age deer is by using their teeth. Enamel on deer teeth is not replaced, so biologists can look at the amount of wear on a deer's teeth to determine age. Dissecting a tooth to look at annual growth layers gives biologists an even more accurate age than surface wear. Unless you get one willing to set in a dentist's chair, deer must be either tranquilized or harvested to obtain an accurate age.

Chapter 9

....

Are You Ready?

ranny, grab your gun! This amusing quote sure is catchy, but responsible hunters don't just grab a gun and head into the woods. Deer hunting requires lots of preparation, and in many cases, the success rate of a hunter will depend on the thoroughness of their preparation.

Sighting in rifles, preseason scouting and even exercising to better their physical condition helps hunters prepare for the rigors of a fall deer season. All these preparations are oriented toward formulating a plan for an upcoming season. The plan's goal is to enrich hunting success and in most cases that means harvesting a nice buck.

Once a plan is in place, it's time to focus on action. Mentally preparing for the moment when that trophy buck appears is fine, but it doesn't do any good if appropriate actions don't follow. Speaking of action, let me share a legendary hunting tale about one of our treasured family members named Jeff.

Jeff was a good hunter who usually harvested a buck or two every year, and occasionally a big one. Since everyone in my family grew up still hunting (stalking), seldom were deer drives ever used. However, during this particular year, dry leaves had made still hunting conditions tough, so on the last day of the season a drive was organized.

Jeff and three other family members were posted as "watchers" while three of us younger participants were to drive deer out of a thick patch of woods. Having drawn the best stand, Jeff shuddered with excitement. Unfortunately, anticipation wasn't the only thing making Jeff wiggle, as that familiar rumbling in his stomach was telling him it was time to deal with that spicy sausage gravy Grandma served that morning.

Jeff struggled to suppress the urge, because he was trying to watch for deer, but with each wiggle Jeff grew more desperate. Finally, thinking that no deer were coming his way, he succumbed to nature's calling. Jeff set his gun beside a tree, dropped his trousers and settled behind a large oak tree. Jeff had just started "getting down to business" when a massive buck came ripping out of the thicket right through his shooting zone. I happened to come out of the thicket just as the action was starting and this is what I witnessed.

The monster buck raced past Jeff as showers of toilet paper flew through the air. I started to lift my rifle, but was paralyzed by the sight of Jeff's white shining bottom which stood between me and the buck. Jeff dived head first into a snow bank grasping for his rifle (I swear he looked just like a pelican diving into the water for a fish). After gaining possession of the gun, Jeff automatically dropped into a "sitting while using the knee for a rest position," forgetting that his trousers were wrapped around his ankles. Jeff's efforts netted him a flash of the buck's tail as the monster disappeared over the hill without Jeff firing a single shot.

Jeff's luck couldn't have been worse as I came down the hill laughing hysterically. The buck ran right over him, all his toilet paper was ruined, his pants were completely soaked and an eyewitness saw the whole affair. To say this was the height of embarrassment for Jeff's hunting career is a major understatement. I still recall that priceless moment when I was rolling on the ground laughing and Jeff pleaded with me never to tell anyone about the incident. Don't worry Jeff, your secret is safe with me.

Although Jeff's "pants incident," as it has now become known, still causes me to break out in hysterical laughter, it brings up a much more serious topic. Just like the appearance of that monster buck, we never know when the opportunity to share God's word will pop up. We need to be ready to act when that opportunity arises, because without proper action, the opportunity may disappear forever. How can we prepare for that moment right now?

1. Practice

   Just like target practice helps to sharpen our shooting skills, the more we practice sharing God's word, the more polished we become. This doesn't mean we need to give sermons in front of our family and friends. Sharing in fellowship, paying attention in church, and discussing God's word with our colleagues will suffice.

2. Different situations require different methods

   One thing that makes hunting trophy bucks so challenging is that most of the time normal hunting techniques just won't do. Specialized strategies must be utilized to consistently harvest trophy bucks, and each hunt requires a unique approach. Likewise, no single person will be able to share God's word with everybody, because different people respond to different styles and personalities.

In 1 Cor. 9, Jesus talks about becoming like the people he witnesses to, in order to be more effective in communicating with them. We don't possess the ability to attract people like Jesus did, but we can do our part by talking to the people that share our common interests. Amazingly, God capitalizes on each individual's unique character in order to share His word with others of similar persona. Regardless of our abilities, God promises to provide strength and know how if we are willing to help spread His word.

3. God's word is mighty

Every day we see fancy products and new techniques that claim they will make us better hunters. But in reality, practice and preparation are the real ingredients that refine our hunting skills, not imitations or new fangled equipment. When witnessing for Christ, no method or technique will have the same effect as God's word. Hebrews 4:12 tells us, *"God's word is quick and powerful and sharper than any two-edged sword, piercing even to the dividing asunder of soul and spirit . . . and is a discerner of the thoughts and intents of the heart."* Use all the creativity you want, but make sure that it centers around God's word, because nothing is more effective.

4. Prayer

How many times have you spotted a nice buck in the brush and started praying "Oh

God, just let him take one more step into
the open?" As hunters, we should be used to
praying. Jesus promises in Heb. 13:5 that *He
will never leave us nor forsake us*, so we are
never alone. God can help in any situation,
and prayer is a direct avenue to ask for His
assistance. Praying for guidance about when
to share God's word can open doors which
were previously closed. The prayer line remains open, and God is always listening.

Hey, we all get scared thinking about witnessing
to other people. What if someone asks a question
we can't answer? What if we mess up? When do we
bring up the topic of God? There are no magical
answers to these questions, but I do know that God's
timing is perfect. Trusting in God and preparing for
a witnessing opportunity can mean the difference
between someone spending eternity with God or
burning in hell.

When a trophy buck comes through the cross-
ing or an opportunity to share God's word opens
up, let's get ready because we sure don't want to get
caught with our pants down.

Fun Facts: The whitetail deer's breeding period
or rut, as it's commonly called, triggers a flurry
of buck activity. Just like antler development,
buck rutting activity is triggered by the production of testosterone. When testosterone levels
reach a certain threshold, bucks know it's time
to start looking for the ladies. Since day length
varies throughout the year, bucks use the amount
of light in a day as an additional rut indicator.
The last variable, and most talked about, is cold
weather. When testosterone levels and day length
are right, a chilly episode can really boost buck
activity.

Chapter 10

. . . .

Tempting Tines

Why do we always want what we don't have? Why does someone else's stuff always seem better? That old adage, "the grass always appears greener on the other side of the fence," often holds true . . . especially if you're hunting near posted property.

While hunting, how many times have you come to a posted boundary fence featuring land on the other side that looked more appealing than your side? I wonder how many times hunters on the other side of that same fence have looked at your property and thought the same thing.

First Cor. 10:13 tells us, *temptation will be common for man, but God will not allow us to be tempted more than we are able to endure and that He will pro-*

vide a way to escape the temptation. Hunting can be a prime arena for temptation because as hunters, we are so passionate about our outdoor accomplishments. We cherish hunting trophies so much that added pressure generated by the threat of failure may persuade us to do unethical things. Like many of us, I'm sure you have felt the urge to cross that posted property fence or shoot a monster buck the week before season opens.

Temptation is one of Satan's most powerful tools, and his efforts are timed impeccably. At your most vulnerable moment, Satan will encourage you to shoot that trophy buck a week before the season opens. Satan even helps you rationalize the wrongdoing, suggesting that if you don't shoot the buck, someone else will.

I love being in the woods during the fall and each year one of my favorite events is the start of fall turkey season. Last fall, turkeys had been spotted a week before season on our mountain property, so that's where I headed on opening day. It didn't take long to find the turkeys, but today they were on the wrong side of a posted property fence. The flock walked so close that I could have shot a turkey, retrieved it through the fence and no one would have ever known. What to do?

Man, it was tough not to pull the trigger on those turkeys as I watched them disappear deeper into the posted land. I have to admit that the gun's safety was clicked on and off a couple of times.

Continuing on the hunt, I headed towards one of my favorite hunting spots and had just crossed over the ridge top when some deer appeared near a dense greenbrier thicket. As I scanned for a better look at the deer, a monster buck burst through the thicket and stopped right in front of me. Only 20 yards separated us and I could easily count the nine large points on his rack without looking through my scope.

Talk about temptation. Sweat ran down my forehead as Satan cast those taunting temptation lines: *Someone else will kill it before season, you'll never see it again, and go ahead-no one will know*. Satan always knows when to turn up the heat.

Think you're the only one who has to deal with temptation? Think again. Whether it's the property fence issue or making a split second decision about harvesting a trophy animal prior to season, tempting situations come suddenly and usually when hunters are not expecting them. Remember, Satan is an effective strategist, and he knows when to apply temptation.

The better we understand temptation, the more apt we'll be to handle it properly. It is important to realize that everyone will encounter temptation. Even Jesus was subjected to 40 days of severe temptation in the wilderness. Exemplifying his master strategist persona, Satan waited until Jesus was tired, hungry and in a very vulnerable position before offering Him the Kingship over all the earth. But Jesus knew that ruling the entire earth was not worth the price of His soul (Luke 4:1–13).

By using temptation, Satan tries to trick us into feeling as if we are doing bad things. Understand that it is not a sin to be tempted and temptation will play a role in each of our lives.

No victory is without opposition and our victory through Christ will not come without struggles. I have heard it stated that temptation is an obstacle on the path of righteousness, and during the course of a lifetime all of us will experience our share of battling through those obstacles.

SOURCES OF TEMPTATION AND HOW TO FIGHT THEM

1. **World** – Pride, money and fame give the outward appearance of being more lucrative than living the selfless Christian way. Faith is the key to countering worldly temptation. You need to have strong faith to live God's way rather than focusing on the world's definition of riches. *"Faith cometh by hearing and hearing by the word of God"* (Rom 10:17).

Reading your Bible, attending church and fellowshipping with Christians are great ways to build faith against the world's foolish philosophy.

2. **Devil** – God tells us that we must stand against Satan, even though he is very powerful. The key will be keeping up our diligence, even when things go bad. We know Satan attacks when we are at our weakest. Studying scripture and spending time in prayer are great ways to counter Satan's efforts. Also, Satan hates to hear about the blood of Jesus, so the next time you feel like Satan is attacking, exploit his weakness by focusing on the blood of Jesus. Just like that famous old hymn claims, there is "Power in the Blood." The day we accept Christ as our Savior, we experience victory over Satan. It is recorded in the Bible that God will crush Satan and his followers and cast them into the lake of fire when the time is right.

3. **Flesh** – Love of the body, lust, sex, drugs and alcohol are very prevalent in our society today. This type of sin seems to ruin more lives than any other. Let's face it, our bodies were born to sin and many of us are really good at it. God tells us to simply flee from fornication and sins of the flesh. In fact, He says to run! When God says to stand up to Satan, one of the most powerful beings ever, but orders us to run from the sins of the flesh, it

certainly indicates how addictive and powerful temptations of the flesh can be.

By understanding temptation and using the
proper tools, we can respond the right way when
faced with tempting choices. Temptation can crush
us or it can make us stronger. Each time we overcome temptation and choose the direction that God
wants us to, we gain confidence and become closer
to God. The closer you become with God, my friend,
the better your life will be.

Fun Facts: Whitetail deer can reach sexual maturity when they are less than a year old. Whitetail populations in most states will not breed until they are 1.5 years old, but early sexual maturing, called "fawn breeding," is profoundly influenced by population density. Higher deer numbers lead to a low percentage of fawn breeding. Consequently, low deer densities can result in a high percentage of fawns that participate in the breeding process, especially during late estrus cycles.

Chapter 11

Do I Have To?

Life can be pretty rough when everyone is your boss. Growing up, how many times did you utter the familiar phrase, "Do I have to, Dad?" As children, we didn't understand all those seemingly silly things that our parents made us do. Those "silly" things usually served an important purpose, but as kids we didn't see it.

When I was eight years old, I can recall listening to every word my dad said. Whatever he said was 100% right. When Dad talked about hunting, I paid particular attention because I was one hunting-crazed kid.

As my teen years erupted, a funny thing happened. A sudden surge of confidence and hunting success fell upon me, and all at once I felt that the things Dad taught me wouldn't work as well as new-age hunting techniques. Dad's way seemed old-fashioned and out of date. Surely, nobody hunts that way anymore.

You had to learn fast in my family because they were constantly on the move. You see, the entire clan was a pack of still hunters. They "stalked" game instead of using more common methods like driving, treestand hunting or stump hunting (so named because hunters employing this technique seemed more interested in staking out their stump than hunting). The skills needed to stalk big game are fairly demanding, but the challenge is exciting and necessary skills can be developed with practice. Still hunters must pay close attention to wind direction, feeding habitats and reading sign (scat, tracks, scraps, etc.) in order to develop the ability to spot game before it detects you.

I justified my shift from Dad's way to the "new" way by assuring myself that modern hunting methods had to be better than the "old school" because of all the new information produced by present day deer research. After all, Scent-Lok clothing and Bio-logic food plots were foreign concepts to my father.

After a few "dry" hunts, it didn't take very long to realize that I had made a mistake in forsaking my father's teaching. Thank goodness I hadn't completely forgotten the "old" way and I soon renewed my affiliation with Dad's time-proven hunting methods, which were based on rock-solid science. Some of those "silly" instructions Dad handed out were starting to make sense.

I am surely glad Dad was patient with me because through the learning process I really tested his patience. Parenting is tough and we all try hard to get our kids to follow proper etiquette, but even as adults we have a tendency not to listen to our Heavenly Father. In the Bible, God specifically outlines guidelines for living that we are supposed to follow. God gives us stories and pictures to illustrate His teaching so that people from different nationalities and time periods can understand the same directives. Never has there been a book that has stood the test of time like the Bible, but we still don't obey it all the time. Why not?

For some reason the ancient phrase "out with the old and in with the new" seems to be too tempting for us to resist. When one of God's rules pop up that we don't like, we catch ourselves uttering those familiar words, "Dad, do I have to?" Imagine how silly it sounds to God when grown adults continue to ask the same question as they did in the fourth grade?

Many people view the Bible as a book of "no-nos" with very strict rules, but the Bible is full of God's wonderful promises and encouragements. No promise is greater than the one in Rom. 10:13 which guarantees that *"Whosoever calleth on the name of the Lord shall be saved."*

Why did your dad instruct you to do so many "silly" things? Was he completely crazy? Of course not, although at times dads can go a little "overboard." Plain and simple, your dad was trying to protect you.

Four reasons dads tell us to do "silly" things:

1. They love us;
2. They want us to avoid trouble;
3. They don't want us to make the same mistakes they did;
4. They want what's best for our lives.

Our Heavenly Father tells us to do seemingly "silly" things for many of the same reasons as our earthly father did. The parallels between the two fathers are striking. God gives us the Bible to help us direct our lives so we can live life to the fullest. By following God's directions, lots of problems and harmful situations can be avoided.

Unlike a dictator, God gives us the freedom to follow His directions or not. It is our responsibility to make the right choices. I know people don't like rules or guidelines and some feel that they will miss out on lots of the fun things in life by conforming to God's rules. I felt that way at one time too, but boy was I wrong!

By following God's guidelines, we get to experience a thousand times more joy and happiness than we ever could by following our own desires. Lots of people have tried to experience more fun on their own instead of following God's rules, but none have ever succeeded.

Next time you hear a child say, "Do I really have to?" Remember that just like that child, we have a set of God-given guidelines to live by. Ultimately God knows best, and yes, we must obey all of his rules. But by following God's guidelines, our lives will be happier than we ever imagined. If you don't believe me, give God a try and see for yourself.

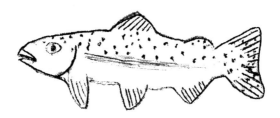

Fun Facts: Catch and release regulations are designed to protect trophy fish and to allow each fish to be caught multiple times. Slot limits are used when small fish are overabundant and the population starts to become stunted. Slots are designed to protect some of the larger fish and encourage harvest of the smaller ones. Size limits are used when anglers over harvest a certain species of fish. Size restrictions are set up to protect fish below a certain size to insure that individual fish have a chance to reproduce before reaching harvestable size.

Chapter 12

Attention Anglers - Special Regulations Ahead

T he enormous shadow loomed just beneath the surface. A flash of silver and my fly disappeared into a large telltale ring. That's all I needed to see before lifting my fly rod high into the air. Well, that sent the show into motion as a frantic rainbow rocketed through the air and put on a dazzling display of aerial somersaults for my fellow anglers up and down the stream.

Overcome with pride and feeling just a bit cocky since I was the only angler catching any trout, I decided to display my angling skills by landing this lunker in midstream instead of a traditional shoreline landing.

Any angler will tell you that fighting a wild rainbow in swift current is a challenge, but landing and unhooking one is such conditions is quite loco. During this particular episode, my fly line became tangled around my waders as the rainbow raced up and down the stream. Doing what I'm sure resembled a clumsy version of the hokey-pokey, I managed to lose my balance.

My body was engulfed in a rush of cold mountain water as I tumbled into the stream. The tippet snapped setting the trout on a freedom run and the mountain side erupted in a chorus of howling laughter as my fellow anglers applauded the makeshift dance routine. That speck of cockiness rapidly transformed into a batch of humble pie, and even I had to chuckle at the turn of events.

During this outing, I'd been trout fishing in one of West Virginia's popular catch and release areas. Several special regulation areas have been established across the state to provide high quality fishing opportunities, and boy, do these places ever offer extraordinary fishing!

However, anglers are required to follow more stringent rules than in normal fishing areas. When anglers abide by these special rules, they reap the benefits of fishing in superb waters. Anglers who aren't willing to follow the rules will never get to participate in such an amazing fishing escapade.

Sound like the Christian life? Critics say there are too many rules, but if you obey God's regulations, you get to reap the benefits that the Lord has in store for you. If you aren't willing to follow God's rules, you'll never experience the full effect of His "special" rewards.

The special regulation areas that don't reach full potential are obvious, and usually it's because people don't obey the entire set of regulations. They abide by some of the rules, but not all. Incomplete compliance prohibits the areas from providing top-notch fishing. To have an effective special regulation area, anglers must obey all the regulations.

Regulation signs which clearly outline the rules anglers are supposed to obey are posted all around the area. God posts his regulations as well, only they aren't on a poster but in a book called the Bible.

In the Bible, God specifically points out a set of special regulations called the Ten Commandments. But today, these sacred documents are viewed as more of a historical work than a directive from God. Many people feel that the commandments are out of date and couldn't possibly be meant for present day living. Something written thousands of years ago surely couldn't apply to modern day life.

Like many of God's directives, the main purpose of the Ten Commandments is to draw our attention to God. Following the Ten Commandments helps to lead us closer to Christ, but observing the Ten Commandments alone will not get us into heaven.

God sent Jesus as a perfect sacrifice for our sin, and the only way to heaven is through Him.

FOUR IMPORTANT DETAILS ABOUT THE TEN COMMANDMENTS:

1. They're a package deal. You can't obey nine of the ten and expect things to be okay. Breaking one is essentially disobeying all ten. Many times we strongly agree with eight or nine, but think we can ignore the rest. Silly us.
2. They show us how much we need salvation. Imagine trying to get to heaven by being sinless. Only with the help of Jesus will we be able to enter into heaven.
3. They are another roadblock to hell. God uses the Ten Commandments to get our attention and as a reminder that we need to accept Jesus. The Bible is very plain when it points out that those who don't accepted Jesus are going to spend eternity in hell.
4. They serve as guidelines for life. Yes, even in today's modern era, the Ten Commandments function as a good guide for living. They don't tell us everything about Christian living that we need to know, but if we obey them, we'll have a very solid foundation on which to build.

Broken a few rules in your time, have you? Well, join the crowd. Okay, so the rule-breaking club is not exclusive. At one time or another, we have all broken the Ten Commandments. The part about honoring our mother and father alone gets all of us (Exodus 20).

The question remains, what can we do about our sinning problem? Simple. We confess our sins to God and do our best not to commit those sins again. God says that *all sins, except one (blasphemy), are forgivable and with His help we can overcome them* (1 John 2:1,2).

However, sins have consequences, and nowhere does God say that overcoming them will be easy. All sin is bad, but serious sins like adultery usually lead to more severe consequences.

With the divorce rate near 50% and immorality at a record level, it's not surprising that sins involving adultery and fornication are seemingly everywhere. Each day, we are literally blasted with images, impressions and examples of improper behavior. It's easy to ignore the rules and enter the danger zone without even realizing it. At present, I would guess that Satan uses this area of sin more than any other to bring down Christians and to keep sinners from experiencing God.

When a person is caught up in the adultery arena, it influences every aspect of their life. Family, finances, physical well-being and overall happiness are ravaged. Family members and friends also experience the horrors. Notice how one little transgression can devastate a large number of people.

For special regulations to be effective on a trout stream, all regulations must be obeyed. Although we like to pick and choose which of God's rules to follow, that's a surefire path to trouble. If you want to experience God's extraordinary benefits, then obey all of His special regulations.

Fun Facts: Florida Bass are not a new species, but a separate strain of the northern largemouth bass. Florida strain largemouth are very popular among anglers because they grow faster, live longer and spawn earlier than their northern strain counterparts. The world record largemouth stands at 22 pounds 4 ounces and was caught in 1932 from Montgomery Lake, GA. California has produced several 20 pounders over the last few years and could very well be the origin of the next world record.

··

Chapter 13

Catch Any Big Ones?

W hen those crystal blue eyes looked up with that inquisitive look, I knew what was coming. "Daddy, did you catch any big ones?" Whether I'm fishing on a lake for largemouth bass or trout fishing on one of West Virginia's magnificent rivers, when I get home from a fishing trip that's the first question my five-year-old son always asks.

Today, anglers spend more time pursuing trophy fish than ever before, and never has there been such pressure to produce big fish. God has blessed me with the knowledge and ability to catch big fish, and through the years, I have had the fortune to catch some dandies. The question is why have we become so focused on the big ones? Our obsession is so pronounced that even a five-year-old can pick up on it.

At the beginning of my fishing career, I needed to catch fish on every trip to be happy. But as my fishing skills became sharper, I evolved into an angler who had to catch a big fish on each trip in order to satisfy my expectations. Although still competitive as ever, I have now matured to a point where I can appreciate multiple aspects of a fishing trip, not just the catching.

No matter how good of an angler you are, there will be times when you will not catch big fish, and maybe you won't catch any fish at all. This can ruin fishing trips if the angler is focused on the prize (fish) rather than the fishing experience.

Maturing as a fisherman teaches the angler to enjoy other aspects of a fishing trip and not just the catching. Time on the water gives you a chance to think about life without everyday pressures of job, family and finances. For many anglers, quiet time on the water becomes an important part of their fishing trip, and the peace they experience while fishing is something that no other activity gives them.

Sometimes it's just as important to learn from the days when you don't catch any big ones as the days when you catch many. How can that be, you ask? Fishing success can be maximized by analyzing weather conditions, fishing pressure, time of year, and moon faze, etc. of days when you blank. Then simply avoid similar conditions in the future. With a limited amount of time to spend on the water, smart anglers want to use it wisely. Knowing which conditions to fish in can make your days on the water much more productive. Targeting favorable conditions rather than wasting time on unproductive ones helps make every minute on the water more rewarding.

Spreading God's word can be just like an unproductive fishing trip. You spend time witnessing, but can't seem to land the big one (see results of your efforts). We often make the mistake of assuming we're not catching any big ones if we don't actually see people getting saved, but many times we may never see the result of our efforts.

By watching us live the Christian life, studying our actions, or hearing our words or encouragement which we dole out, others may be drawn to the Lord. Standing up for God or taking stands against things we know aren't right can affect people in ways that aren't outwardly evident. However, God always sees our willingness to serve Him, and He uses our abilities in ways that we may never know about. God has the ability to take a little and make a lot. After all, He is God!

We must be careful not to use a "human" ruler to measure the volume of activity that we feel it takes to be a successful Christian. For example, a pastor may lead 100 souls to Christ and you may only lead one, therefore the pastor has done much more than you. A hundred souls is definitely better than one, but realize that the solitary soul you helped save is extremely important. You may be that person's only hope. God may have placed you in a position where no other person on earth is capable of leading that person to Christ. How's that for importance? You have the ability to share information which could determine if a person spends eternity in heaven or hell.

One of the most impressive things about God is that He can use you regardless of your ability. How cool is that? God matches your abilities, no matter how unworthy you think they are, to His service. It never ceases to amaze me how God takes a person's abilities that they consider to be weak and turns them into useful talents.

So, the next time you can't seem to catch any big ones, remember *"All things work together for good to them that love God"* (Rom 8:28). Serving God by doing tasks that you feel have little or no meaning, often lead to magnificent things. You may not see concrete results of your service or influence, but God can do wonders if we just let Him guide our actions.

Give God your availability, and He will work wonders through you. Remember we can't accomplish anything productive without God, so whether you're fishing for souls or largemouth bass, you don't always have to catch big ones to be successful.

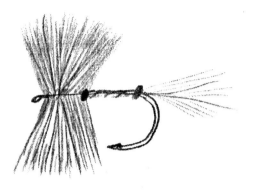

Fun Facts: Several species of trout inhabit the United States, but anglers are most familiar with rainbow, brown, brook and cutthroat. Brown and brook trout are fall spawners which occasionally hybridize creating a cross called a "tiger" trout. Tiger trout are commonly induced in a hatchery setting, but are rare in the wild. Rainbow and cutthroat trout are spring spawners, but they too can hybridize forming a cross called a "cutbow." Unlike tiger trout, cutbows are quite common in wild streams inhabited by both rainbows and cutthroat.

. . . .

Chapter 14

Going on a Trip

Anticipation is a powerful thing. At times it can even be better than the actual experience. Whether or not that's the case for you, planning a fishing or hunting adventure and anxiously waiting for the trip to begin is certainly an important part of the overall experience.

Nothing gets me through those tough winter months better than the anticipation of an upcoming fishing trip. Not only does an angler get to enjoy the actual trip, but they get to experience months of thinking and dreaming about their adventure.

During the anticipation period, excited chatter with sportsmen, friends and family members is often commonplace. It's thrilling to talk about an up-

coming trip and such word-of-mouth inquiries can
provide you with valuable information.

Although some anglers sit idly by waiting for
their trip to begin, I encourage you to really get involved and thoroughly prepare for your next trip.
Trip research is a vital link that can add lots of en-
joyment to your fishing excursion by providing better fishing locations, productive lures, eating spots,
accommodations, and might even save you money.
Preparations made prior to your next trip's departure may quite literally determine the difference
between having an enjoyable trip or one that is ruined because of some oversight.

A great way to prepare for your expedition is to
gather proper equipment, tackle and other items. I
spend hours tying flies for my fly fishing trips, enjoying every minute of it. I like to be involved in
every phase of the trip and having proper equipment can be a real asset in overcoming problems
that may pop up along the way. For example, breaking my fly rod on a trip to Colorado could have resulted in disaster, but since I brought along my Orvis
guarantee card, a local dealer handed me a new rod
across the counter and I was back on the water in
less than an hour.

Another great trip preparation is to brush up on
your casting skills prior to trip departure. Over the
winter, the old casting arm probably got a bit rusty.

A little practice will get you ready to fish upon arrival at the trip destination rather than wasting valuable time working the kinks out. If possible, practice in conditions that will be similar to those you'll encounter during your trip. Maybe even tie a fly line to one of your kids and sprint them across the yard just so you can hear the scream of your reel's drag. On second thought, maybe the kid run is not such a good idea. The kids will love it when you reel them in across a puddle-filled yard, but it will probably be very unpopular with the wife (speaking from first-hand experience).

I fondly recall my last trip to Yellowstone. Accompanied by my father-in-law, we set off on the trip of a lifetime. This journey encompassed both my father-in-law's first trip out west and his first time ever flying on a commercial airline. Talk about anxious anticipation! He turned a little white when the plane lifted off, but as long as he didn't turn green, I knew we were good to go.

We ended up having a wonderful time and my father-in-law can't wait to return to Yellowstone country to catch those magnificent trout again. The entire experience was so spiritual. As we enjoyed some of the world's best fly fishing in such a scenic setting, we couldn't help but feel close to God. Fishing in such a magnificent place really helped us appreciate all that God has done for each of us.

Lots of preparation went into planning that trip and it really paid dividends. We practiced casting, researched hatch charts, river conditions, weather patterns and even upgraded our equipment.

As Christians we look forward with great anticipation to the second coming of Christ (rapture), but there are lots of things we can do to prepare for the trip.

Most important of course, is making sure that we have followed God's plan of salvation. Only by admitting we sin, realizing the penalty for sin is death and accepting Jesus can we escape sin's penalty. Romans 10:9 tells us, *when we verbally claim Jesus as our savior and believe in our heart that God raised Jesus from the dead, we become saved.*

Equipment preparation is a very important step for any trip, especially the one God has in store for us. Find a good church and use it. Become active and utilize the tools that God gave you. Don't tell me you don't have any because God gave us all plenty of top-notch equipment. Mine definitely did not include singing in the choir, but things like working with the youth group or the church softball team fit just fine.

Studying the Bible is similar to researching a trip, although the rewards are much greater. Use study guides, get into a study group, become an active participant in a Sunday school class or whatever else helps you learn more about God's word. Don't just read it, study and memorize God's word like an avid trout fishermen would a Yellowstone hatch chart.

What skills do you need to improve on before embarking on your next trip? Improvements come with practice and the more you practice sharing God's word, the easier it becomes. Get out and tell people about Jesus. On the job, on the ball field, at a family reunion or whatever avenue God provides, plan on sharing His encouragement. Living a proper Christian life like the Bible instructs is an extremely effective way to share God's encouragement. People are always watching Christians, and at any time they might inquire about God.

One day soon, we will be taking the grandest trip of our lives. It won't be to Yellowstone, Alaska or the Bahamas, it will be to heaven. As we wait for Jesus with great anticipation, why not gear up for the trip?

Although nothing can be as magnificent as heaven, when we share our encouragement, study our Bible, work through our church, and of course, follow God's basic plan, we might just experience a little bit of heaven on earth until it's time to take that spiritual trip to the Promised Land.

Fun Facts: Fly fishing for trout with dry flies is very exciting, but 90% of a trout's diet is composed of underwater forage and for good reason. Aquatic insects which trout feed upon spend 95% of their life in aquatic stages (nymphs, pupa, emerger). Certain stonefly species spend nearly three years underwater before emerging for a brief three week period. Mayfly hatches can be even more compressed as each mayfly spends nearly a year in the aquatic form, one to two weeks emerging and only a few hours out of water before dying.

Chapter 15

Gamehogs

Back off a few steps, mister! I couldn't believe the nerve of this guy. Some unscrupulous angler had just cast across my son's fishing line in an attempt to horde in on the five-year-old's fishing spot. Ordinarily, I wouldn't have said anything, but when such an obvious breach of etiquette occurs, it becomes difficult to hold your tongue.

My son and I had been enjoying an afternoon of trout fishing on one of our favorite trout streams when the stock truck arrived. I'm not a big fan of fishing the river on stocking day, because I like to fish for trout that have been acclimated to the stream. However, since Noah was along, I thought it might be good for my son to experience some rapid trout-catching action. It didn't take long for

Noah to catch a trout and we were both elated. After taking a few pictures and relishing the moment, we geared up to try for another. That's when the gamehogs moved in.

I noticed the three scruffy characters creeping closer, but didn't really pay much attention to them. However, as soon as my son hooked his second trout, the gamehogs moved within a few feet of us and started casting into our spot. It completely ruined our fishing experience and when the most aggressive of the gamehogs hooked Noah's line as my son was trying to land his second trout, I issued my stern warning.

Hastily, the gamehogs landed their limit of six trout and would probably have exceeded that limit had we not been there. Unceremoniously, they dumped all the trout in a plastic bag and sped away, leaving my son and I disgusted over the entire incident.

Gamehogs are full of obnoxious tactics which have earned them a ranking among the sporting world's least desirables. Each morning of the trout stocking season, gamehogs actually stakeout state fish hatcheries and follow the stock trucks to each stocking site. They sprint to the water's edge and wait like hungry dogs for the river to be filled with trout. Gamehogs yearn to catch every trout in the stream and their greed causes them to trample any streamside angler which may be in their way. No wonder sportsmen have such a strong distaste for gamehogs.

Why such greed over a few hatchery trout? Unlike a trout that lives in the stream for a while, hatchery fish aren't colorful, nor do they taste good. With somewhat of a bland taste, stockers are nowhere near as flavorful as wild trout. Tender pink fillets of a wild trout serve as an accurate prediction that the ensuing meal is going to taste delicious.

Following the stock truck to catch freshly stocked trout is simply not sporting, and most anglers consider it an appalling practice. State game agencies hear complains about stock truck followers all the time, and numerous management strategies have been implemented to alleviate this predicament. However, when gamehogs stake out trout hatcheries each morning and then follow the stock trucks on public highways, little can be done.

Gamehogs are so focused on catching more fish than other anglers that they don't even appreciate the trout they catch nor do they value the overall fishing experience which true sportsmen cherish. Gamehogs seek quick gratification, and each fish caught is just another meaningless number instead of the trip highlight that it should be.

The bottom line seems to be that gamehogs want all the "good stuff" without earning it. I hate to ad-

mit it, but sometimes church-going folks fall under
the same spell. We want all God's blessings without
the confines of living by His rules. God promises
that if we obey His rules, the "good stuff" will follow. Second Chr. 15:7 tells us, *"Be ye strong therefore, and let not your hands be weak: for your work
shall be rewarded."* But still we covet financial wealth,
a great job, an ideal family, and other benefits without the burden of conforming to a Godly lifestyle.
How silly is that?

We forget that living the Christian lifestyle is
what generates the bounty of "good stuff" in the
first place. Contrary to our distorted view, we don't
get the "good stuff" and then find God, the "good
stuff" is one of the benefits of living God's way.

No matter how hard we try, at times we cease to
give God His due. We stop studying God's word,
attending church regularly, praying or spending de-
votional time with our Creator. Foolishly, we forget
that our bond with God requires a lifelong commitment. We know our relationship with God needs to
strengthen, but along with every other Christian,
we battle the tendency to become lax. If we aren't
careful, we can end up drifting away from God's direction.

The desire for the "good stuff," never ends and
when the "good stuff" becomes scarce, we can't understand why it dried up. Perhaps it might have

something to do with our lifestyle shift. When God becomes a secondary priority in our lives, trouble usually surfaces.

The world demands quick gratification, and without a doubt America leads the world in the search for gratification. From the drive thru at McDonalds to the almost instantaneous access to internet information, we want that quick fix. And watch out when we don't get instant service! Those impatient waits at the doctor's office or the seemingly endless pauses at red lights make us steaming mad. In the grand scheme of things, these "long" waits don't amount to much, but they sure do accelerate our frustration levels. Let's be careful not to become gamehogs in our daily lives, because a quick gratitude mind-set sure can get out of control fast.

The best things in life require diligent work. Working hard to achieve goals gives us great satisfaction, but it only lasts for a short while. As Christians, we have the advantage of knowing everlasting satisfaction (Jesus). Jesus decrees, *"I am the bread of life: he that cometh to me shall never hunger; and he that believeth on me shall never thirst"* John 6:35.

Greed-driven gamehogs will never be able to attain true satisfaction and their self-indulgence will continually result in displays of inappropriate behavior. Sure sounds like a hassle-filled way of life and certainly not the existence I want, either in my outdoor pursuits or everyday living.

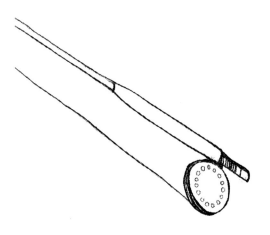

Fun Facts: Pacific sailfish average 80–120 pounds and are much heavier that the Atlantic version which averages 50–80 pounds. The Pacific coast of Central America has become a billfishing hotspot and is one of the few places where anglers can experience year round billfish action. Twenty pound tippet is the heaviest line allowed by IFGA in order to recognize a fly rod catch or establish a world record with a fly.

Chapter 16

. . . .

Mind Games

Wherever the mind goes, the feet will follow. The best way to tackle any problem
is be prepared to handle the problem before it arises. Sounds like something right out of a
psychology textbook, doesn't it?

No matter how you define it, mental preparation is vital to succeeding in many outdoor hunting
or fishing situations. Whether you call it buck fe-
ver, fishing panic or another catchy name, sometimes hunters and anglers get so excited that they
completely fall apart when it matters most. Usually,
the better prepared we are prior to the moment of
truth, the more likely we will be to remain calm and
deal with the circumstances.

Better mental preparation equals superior fishing success, and in many cases, the results speak for themselves. Mental preparation, or the lack of it, certainly played a role in my recent trip to Costa Rica where I battled giant sailfish with a fly rod. Yes, even a mountain boy like me knows about saltwater fly fishing, although for me the sailfish trip was truly a once in a lifetime event and something I had always wanted to do.

I conducted quite a bit of research on Costa Rica sail fishing before I went on the trip, but nothing prepared me for the massiveness of a 100-pound sailfish. I was dumbfounded by the fact that these giant sailfish are teased to within spitting distance of the boat before the fly is presented. Now, I have caught some dandy fish in my time, but when a fish exceeding eight feet comes close enough to touch with the end of the fly rod, I get shook up. Consequently, broken tippet, lost flies, a broken fly rod and other chaos ensued for a time until I got the hang of it.

Having fly fished for many species across the country, I felt prepared to handle sailfish on a fly rod. However, during all my research I forgot to formulate a mental plan of action which would keep me calm when the moment of truth arrived. Developing a fishing strategy is important, and thinking things through before the heat of the moment arrives can mean the difference between success and failure.

Anglers are notorious for putting lots of preparation into their quests, particularly in some of the specialties like fly fishing. But do we put as much effort into spreading God's word as we do preparing for one of those special fishing trips?

Preparing a plan of action helps us to be more effective in spreading God's word, just like a well-organized fishing strategy makes us better anglers. God wants us to prepare ourselves so we can share His message with the same enthusiasm that we would sink into planning a world-class fishing trip. Remember, the more effort we put into preparation, the more likely we are to succeed.

GETTING READY

1. **Know Jesus is the Lord**
   It's essential that you have the utmost confidence that God is the Almighty Creator and Ruler of all. This world started with Him and it will end with Him. The Alpha and the Omega; the beginning and the end. As anglers and hunters who experience the magnificent outdoors up close and personal, we are continually reminded of what a majestic God it took to create all the interactions that make our earth function.

2. **Be ready**

   To be successful, an angler must be ready to set the hook at any instant. Even when we think we're primed for action, sometimes a fish is missed because the hook set wasn't quick enough. Opportunities to witness may also arise quickly, and often they come in unexpected ways. God tells us in 1 Peter 3:15, *"Be ready always to give an answer to every man that asketh you a reason of the hope that is in you."* We need to be ready to inform others about God's greatness. Opportunities may come in many forms because God uses abilities in us that we may not necessarily see as our best attributes. Perhaps, this forces us to focus on God for strength instead of trying to do everything ourselves.

3. **Encouragement**

   Don't get frustrated because your witnessing efforts haven't paid off the way you feel they should. Just because you haven't led anyone to Christ (a mighty feat), or because you haven't led enough souls to Christ, don't think your spiritual endeavors have missed their mark. God assures us in 1 Cor. 3:8 *that every man shall receive rewards for good works even though they may not directly see the results.* Unlike a successful fishing trip where we can see the results of preparation (like a trophy fish mounted on the wall or tasty fillets on the table), the outcome of our Godly service may not be so obvious. We may never know how many people have been influenced by our Christian lives, but God uses our actions, words or even the way we conduct ourselves to glorify His word. Also, be aware that the devil is very good at discouraging those doing God's work. As anglers, we often become frustrated when the fish aren't biting, but usually those who stick with it and keep fishing are the ones who bring home the trophies. Persistence pays off. In Gal. 6:9, God assures us again *that if we keep doing good things, in due time, we shall be rewarded.*

4. **God is in control**

Know that God is guiding and directing our efforts. We can do nothing on our own, but Matt. 19:26 tells us, "*With God all things are possible.*" God wants us to enjoy life, and the Bible informs us that by living God's way we will obtain more joy than any worldly guidance could ever provide. Fishing is one of life's great pleasures that I really enjoy, and if you really want to attract the attention of a non-believer, let them see how much fun living the Christian life is. Whether it's on a fishing trip or in the way God guides us through a difficult problem, show others that it feels awesome when God takes control of our lives. In Matt. 5:16, Jesus tells us to "*Let your light so shine before men, that they may see your good works, and glorify your father which is in heaven."*

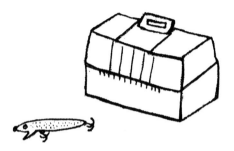

Fun Facts: Smallmouth bass spawn when water temperature reaches 65 degrees F. Females can lay 7,000 eggs per pound of body weight, but it's the males who play a vital role in the reproductive effort. Males guard the nest for two to seven days until the eggs hatch. Males continue to protect the newly hatched fry for an additional week or two while the fry move off the nest to explore their new world. Even with the extra protection, only ten percent of the fry will survive long enough to reach two inches.

. . . .

Chapter 17

Equipment Overload

As the razor-sharp knife sliced left and then right, I peered deep into the black opening. After a layer of soft tissue paper was removed, a gleaming treasure of plastic lures appeared. The glowing smile across my face served as genuine proof that this angler was elated with the contents of this gift.

There must be a point where anglers completely satisfy their need for additional fishing gear, but if such a point exists, I've yet to find it. Along comes a hot new lure and boom, anglers swing into buying mode. Overcome by creative advertising which promises to enhance our angling ability, we simply must acquire that new lure. Just ask my wife. My den is full of such "necessary" gear.

I'm sure you know what I'm talking about: underwater cameras, six ball bearing reels, rattling jigs, senkos in four different sizes, at least a dozen graphite rods, and of course, a whole bunch of the latest 3-D soft plastics that look real enough to swim right out of your tackle box. As modern anglers, we feel obligated to acquire all of these and more. Can't fall behind the times now, can we?

It's scary to think back to the old days when I carried a solitary rod, a pocket-sized tackle box and a pair of fingernail clippers. Simple equipment, but man did I catch a lot of fish that way! Thanks to an accumulation of modern gear, my present day look resembles that of a combat ready marine rather than an angler. I'm sure it makes me look quite ridiculous, but the fear of leaving behind that "necessary" lure will probably keep me overpacking.

Anglers have become obsessed with equipment and gadgets. We rely so heavily on our lures and tackle that some anglers simply won't go onto the water without suitcases full of them. Where will our reliance on this "necessary" gear end?

As Christians, we face a similar dilemma. We ask God for extra equipment (ability, courage, strength) to carry out His assignments because we don't feel adequately equipped to do the job. In reality however, God has given us more than enough stuff to conduct His business. God reassures us in

Prov. 16: 9 that *He would never leave us without the tools to do His will.*

Ever pray for something to really zing up your life? Many times that *zing* is already in our possession, but we just haven't accessed it yet. Realize that God has already given us sufficient skills, and when we use them properly, great things happen. In 2 Cor. 2:14, God tells us that *He always causes us to triumph in Christ.*

However, just possessing built-in tools doesn't mean we know how to operate them. Take anger for instance. We have the ability to control our temper, but some of us really struggle keeping it under wraps. All of us need to hone our skills in order to become more efficient Christians. Just like any builder, the more we work with our tools, the more skilled we become in handling the equipment God gave us.

Whenever you feel ill-equipped to handle a situation, remember God's promise in Joshua 1:5, *"I will be with thee: I will not fail thee, nor forsake thee."* Don't worry about God leaving you high and dry, because He won't. If you're looking for a little supplemental guidance, the Bible serves as somewhat of an owner's manual to help us master our internal equipment. The Bible also functions as a source of strength that we can draw from when confronting life's everyday affairs.

Don't think you're alone when you feel insufficiently equipped to handle a difficult task. The Bible is full of great characters who felt more than a little inadequate when God assigned them duties. Moses whined like a fourth grader and gave God a ton of excuses in an effort to escape his assignment. Gideon felt so unprepared that he hid from God. Jonah tried to leave the country, and dear old Paul spent most of his life "sick as a dog." But, God used each of these fellows to carry out major accomplishments in the Bible. Can you imagine doing something so grand that it earned you a place in God's Hall of Fame (Hebrews 11)? These hesitant Christians all felt that they didn't possess the right stuff to complete God's assignments, but by trusting in Him, not only did they discover the proper equipment within themselves, they learned how to use it effectively.

When we trust in God, He helps us to uncover tools and abilities deep within us. What great gifts dwell inside of you that God is waiting to utilize?

Fun Facts: Brook trout remain the most common native trout species in the eastern United States while cutthroat are native to much of the western portion of our country. Brown trout traveled a long way to reach our country as these prized gamefish originated in Germany. Brown trout can tolerate warmer water temperatures than other trout, thus allowing them to thrive in slower moving streams and lakes where other trout species cannot.

....

Chapter 18

Not Now, I'm Busy

It was a perfect day. Spring's initial warm snap had initiated the river's first really good hatch of the year. What more could a trout enthusiast ask for? Anticipating a day of dynamite trout fishing, I could hardly wait to hit the water after such a long cold winter. My friend, Nick, and his dad, Marlin, were to join me on this trout fishing adventure, but when the appointed meeting time arrived, no one showed up. I waited for nearly 30 minutes before heading to the river alone.

Fishing was every bit as good as anticipated and hungry trout were slamming my dry flies as they bounced on top of the rolling current. I can't remember how many trout I caught that morning, but the number was certainly impressive.

Other than garnering a bruised butt when I attempted a spectacular pirouette on some slippery river rocks, the morning was absolutely delightful. I wished my friends could have enjoyed the experience as well, but I wondered what could have kept them away?

Both were avid outdoorsmen and since this was the first notable trout fishing opportunity of the year, they had to be chomping at the bit to get on the river just like me. Later that afternoon, the would-be anglers finally showed up.

The morning hatch had already passed, and consequently, fishing during the afternoon was not nearly as productive. The bite had passed and fishing was sub par compared to the frenzied trout-catching action during the morning hatch.

Nick was very disappointed at missing the season's first hatch and I couldn't blame him, but Marlin was chipper as usual. You see, Marlin loved to hunt and fish as much as anyone, but he was always willing to help out those in need. That morning a needy soul experienced an emergency repair, which had to be fixed.

Since Marlin happened to be a top-notch building contractor who could build or fix just about anything, people called for help often. All that helping hand stuff added up to a lot of missed hunting and fishing time over the years, but Marlin never seemed to mind. He was always smiling and his positive demeanor was instantly contagious. Even when situations looked hopeless, Marlin's easy joking manner and helpful attitude served as a reassuring presence to everyone. Countless outdoor opportunities were missed because many of these helping hand efforts overlapped with prime hunting and fishing periods, but Marlin never complained. What a Godly example he set!

It is pretty much inevitable that problems will arise at the most inopportune times. If you don't believe me just add a couple of kids to the mix. Even if you find a way to avoid the urgent ringing of the phone, odds are that one of your kids will arrange a sudden trip to the emergency room, set an untimely fire or even worse, give you the famous sad eye look and say, "Daddy, I wanna go fishing too." Cheerful conduct is probably not the first thing that comes to mind as you put away your favorite bass rods and get out the Snoopy poles and bobbers.

Most of us are familiar with the phrase "time is money," but I believe time spent outdoors is much more important than money. My hunting and fishing time is sacred and without it, I feel unfulfilled. However, when you are willing to give up your precious time to help another, God is pleased. God says giving is good, and I don't know of anything more valuable to give than your time, especially if it's those cherished outdoor moments.

God has a way of rewarding those who help others. Luke 6:38 says "Give (unto others) and it shall be given unto you." Additional benefits abound from those whom we help. Where I grew up, people helped each other all the time, and favors were returned when folks seemed to need them the most. Countless times when something bad happened and things looked bleak, troublesome situations were remedied by neighbors helping neighbors. If you want to enrich your life, try helping someone in need, regardless of the sacrifices you might have to make.

The last time I applied this advice, I received access to an awesome fishing spot. Typically, an elderly lady called to request some assistance during an afternoon that I had planned to spend fishing. Even though she and her husband lived quite a distance away, I decided to forego my afternoon of fishing to help her out. I'm usually more selfish with my hunting and fishing time than this, and I'm still not sure what motivated me that day.

After providing the necessary assistance, the lady asked what I had planned for the day, and I told her of my scheduled fishing trip. She said, "You know, I have a little old pond over the hill that no one fishes. It isn't much, but you are welcome to try it." Since my fishing gear was already packed in the truck and it was too late to reach my initial destination anyway, I said okay, probably more to keep from disappointing the lady than anything else.

Well now let me tell you, when I came around the hill and saw the pond, it looked like the gates of heaven! The lady's pond was absolutely gorgeous and more importantly, full of giant largemouth. Bass fishing that afternoon was incredible and after catching my third trophy bass from the pond, I thought to myself that God always comes through. When we give a little of ourselves to help someone, God sees that we are rewarded. Whether we reap the benefits here on earth or one day in heaven, rest assured God never loses track of our good deeds. Take care of God's work and He will take care of providing for your wants and needs. You can never out give God.

I'm still stingy with my hunting and fishing time, and I'll never be as giving with my time as Marlin was, but his example sure helps us realize how great helping others can be.

Marlin's life was shortened by a crippling disease, and the Lord called him home long before many of us were ready to see him go, but who are we to second guess God's timing. Maybe God just needed a little help fixing a leaky pipe and everyone else was busy.

Fun Facts: Fish "hear" by detecting vibrations in the water through their lateral line in the same manner that human ears pick up sound waves traveling through the air. The lateral line consists of a series of scales running from the tail to the gill plate. Each scale has a tiny opening full of sensitive nerve endings. With lateral lines on both sides, not only does the fish detect vibrations, but it can pinpoint the vibration's origin.

Chapter 19

Have a Good Day

Escape was my only hope. Pressures from job, family and worldly stress can really build up, and a fabulous way to relieve the escalating tension is through fishing. The gentle rocking of a boat against a lake's rippling chop just seems to calm my soul. Of course, I'm not just sitting on my duff, I'm fishing. The plop of a Texas-rigged worm as it rockets downward through the lake's surface serves as music to my ears. The hassles of the world are driven out of my mind as I attentively wait for the subtle thump of my line that indicates a mighty largemouth has just engulfed the soft worm.

Early in my fishing career, I often found myself fishing alone, but one day I made a surprising discovery: fishing with a friend can be loads of fun.

Besides providing lively conversation, fishing partners add lots of intangible benefits to a trip. Fishing partners share information and fishing tips; help record memorable catches on film; stretch the truth of those infamous fishing tales; laugh about mishaps and share in the elation when a trophy bass is landed. Plain and simple, fishing is more enjoyable with a partner. Angler surveys across the country indicate that spending time with friends/fishing partners is one of the most significant reasons why anglers fish.

Tournament anglers know better than anyone just how valuable a good fishing partner can be. Serious camaraderie and trust develop between two anglers when they share a common goal and usually teams who win consistently are the ones that really enjoy fishing together. Even though disagreements pop up at times, established fishing partners share a special bond that extends way beyond fishing.

Largemouth bass have become one of my favorite fishing quarries and I fish for them every chance I get, whether my fishing partner is along or not. But I discovered long ago that trips which include a fishing partner are usually more fun than solo ventures. This is particularly true when fishing is on the extreme ends of the success spectrum.

On days when the action is superb, you want someone to share the enthusiasm and be a part of the fabulous fishing experience. Besides, when the bass bite is hot, a solitary angler can never catch them all and an extra angler helps put more fish in the boat. Partners also provide another voice to embellish those legendary fishing tales and any time two voices sing the same song, it helps to validate the story. Surely, anglers wouldn't stretch a fishing story to fictional proportions, would they?

A good partner might be most valuable on days when the fishing is slow. Swapping stories, passing along hot fishing tips and recalling funny mishaps can turn an ordinary day into a satisfying fishing experience. Partners possess a magical ability to convert "average" into "EXCEPTIONAL."

Plus, partners share expenses. Bait, tackle, lodging and gas expenses can all be reduced by half. Not a bad thing when operating on a tight budget like most of us.

When I initially started catching lots of big bass, greed reared its ugly head and I wanted to keep all the action for myself. I still love the action, but the first time I took an old friend on one of my fishing adventures, a peculiar thing happened. I actually enjoyed coaching him through his first big bass encounter almost as much as if I were catching the bass myself.

My favorite time to bass fish occurs when big bass move into shallow water to spawn. Sight fishing for giant bass in skinny water is the ultimate in bass fishing as far as I'm concerned, and at the very least it's exhilarating. I remember watching the concentration and pure delight etched on my partner's face as he cast to his first monster bass. My friend had never seen bass this large before so veteran anglers know very well the excitement my partner experienced during that inaugural fishing trip. Of course, preliminary jubilation can be followed by frustration when bass won't bite or line breakages occur. Plenty of mishaps occurred over the years, but the point is each of our adventures, good or bad, was enhanced by the addition of a fishing partner.

My old friend quickly became a bass fishing addict and has since developed into my premier fishing partner. Together, we enjoy countless hours on the water each year. Looking back upon our resume, some of our fishing trips turned out to be terrible while others earned phenomenal ratings, but I can honestly say each trip was better because we fished together.

Any day an angler spends on the water is a good day, but why settle for good when you could have great? God wants each day that we spend on this earth to be great, and with His help it can happen.

Among anglers, there seems to be no closer friend than a fishing partner. Fishing partners are with us through thick and thin. Together, we experience the thrill of tournament victories, and the agony of defeat when each mighty bass is lost. Through the ups and downs, a strong relationship is formed that has a way of making the good times a little better and the bad times not so bad.

WHAT FRIENDS GIVE US:

1. Harmony - When we start complaining about every little thing, being contrary or simply losing focus, friends help get us back on the right track and prevent us from becoming sidelined by minuscule problems. 1 Peter 3:10–11 tells us, *To refrain from evil and let our lips speak no guile . . . do good, seek peace and ensue it.* Without little reminders and some sound guidance, insignificant annoyances can blossom into major troubles.
2. Compassion - When necessary, friends are there to comfort us. Sometimes just listening as we unload a problem by getting it "off our chest" can be a huge help. During hard times, it is often friends that provide the most comfort.
3. Love - I'm referring to brotherly love, not the romantic kind. True friendship forms a bond strong enough for friends to support

each other no matter what. Proverbs 17:17 says, *"A friend loveth at all times, and a brother is born for adversity."*

4. Respect - This sometimes means being honest. Honesty can hurt, but it keeps us from being superficial. Understanding the outdoor lifestyle and being able to share it with others generates mutual respect. It's nice to know people enjoy some of the same outdoor activities that we do and respect us for who we really are.

5. Be courteous - Friends serve as a reminder to not always think of ourselves, but of others. We feel comfort when friends look after our well being, and it helps us to pass along the same courtesy to others.

Humans are social critters designed to seek companionship. Sharing fishing experiences with a friend can be a great way to enhance our precious treasured outdoor time that we enjoy so much. Sometimes your partner might serve as a teacher, a student or just a teammate; either way having a good companion along can turn a good fishing trip into a great one.

Next time someone asks if you're having a good day, look over at your fishing partner and tell them no, you're having a great day . . . just like God intended.

Fun Facts: Bass have an incredible ability to pinpoint their home territories. Bass captured in fishing tournaments and scientific tag studies have been known to swim more than 15 miles back to their original capture locations. How this "homing" sense works remains a mystery to scientists. Hundreds of documented incidents where bass traveled great distances to return to their home locations leaves little doubt that a bass' built-in GPS works very well.

* *

Chapter 20

Don't Step on the Little Guy

Racing down the lake at neck-break speed, we nearly ran over the small johnboat before we saw him. A frantic jerk of the wheel provided the evasive action we needed to avoid a collision, but our boat's trailing wake almost capsized the small johnboat. Once again, I cautioned my partner to slow down, but all he could focus on was finishing among the top ten in today's regional bass tournament. Such a feat would earn him a spot in the national finals.

I felt bad for the small johnboat, but the damage had already been done. We would probably never see the boat again anyway.

Running his 225 Mercury wide open, my partner headed for a cove on the lower end of the lake.

This cove was reputed to contain several lunker bass and that's what we desperately needed to catch.

Fishing was good, but most of the bass we caught barely measured above the 12-inch minimum length. A six fish limit came quickly, but the overall size of our catch remained in question. We had fished our cove exclusively for nearly 45 minutes when we spotted another boat puttering toward us. Attempting to claim the best fishing location, my partner raced his imposing boat across the cove in an attempt to cut off the newcomer.

Seemingly oblivious to my partner's rude maneuver, the small boat turned into the cove and motored over to the shoreline we had just vacated. As the boat passed, we recognized it as the small johnboat we had nearly crashed into earlier that morning. The angler's water-soaked jacket and pants served as proof that our high speed flyby had indeed inflicted causalities.

The angler in the small boat hadn't fished for more than ten minutes before catching his first bass, and it was a big one. My partner muttered something about blind luck, but when that same angler landed his second five-pound bass from the exact spot we had just fished, my partner became agitated.

Tossing aside all ethical courtesy, my partner crowded back into the location where "Mr. Johnboat" (as the angler in the small craft had been deemed) was fishing. Mr. Johnboat didn't say a word to my partner as the old guy was shamefully driven from his fishing area. I was thoroughly embarrassed and told my partner so, but all reason had been shoved aside as he obsessed over his tournament quest.

Mr. Johnboat strolled across the cove to where we had just been and reestablished his fishing routine. Just then one of the tournament officials came motoring down the lake and stopped by our boat. He reported that lots of big bass were being caught from the other side of the lake and several teams had already racked up hefty limits.

With this new information, my partner really began to feel the pressure. To finish within the top ten, my partner realized he would need to add some big bass to our tally. As we pondered the situation, Mr. Johnboat landed another bass, and this one was a giant, probably pushing seven pounds or more.

Desperation drove my partner over to Mr. Johnboat and a ton of pride was swallowed as my veteran companion humbly asked the small boat angler for some assistance. Mr. Johnboat looked up with an amused expression and began to speak.

Sounding like a cross between a Baptist minister and a college professor, Mr. Johnboat lectured my partner for the next ten minutes. During the eloquent verbal oratory, he confronted my partner about his inappropriate behavior. The old guy didn't miss a thing, thoroughly covering rudeness, ethics, greed and uppityness. My partner felt so ashamed by the conclusion of the sermon that he woefully uttered a weak apology and prepared to accept defeat when a surprising development emerged.

Mr. Johnboat followed up his lecture by informing my partner that since his apology seemed sincere the old guy would now be willing to help. Capitalizing on the priceless information from Mr. Johnboat, my partner went on to claim the tenth and final spot in the tournament, thus earning a trip to the national finals.

This memorable outing shares many similarities with Genesis' familiar account of Joseph. Joseph's life story offers many virtuous principles for us to examine and apply to our lifestyles.

The part of the story where Joseph's brothers appeared before him in Egypt serves as proof that you should never step on the "little guy." At the time of his abduction, Joseph was just an ordinary person, but by the time the brothers appeared before him in Egypt, Joseph ranked as the second most powerful person in all the land. The source of Joseph's pain and agony, his so-called brothers, now stood before Joseph entirely at his mercy.

But Joseph displayed the same characters as Mr. Johnboat did on that unforgettable tournament day.

In Gen. 42:7, we see that Joseph harshly confronted his brothers, but he wasn't angry with them. Joseph wanted his brothers to realize they had done wrong and to make sure of their sincerity before giving them the food they wanted. Even before Joseph revealed his identity, we see the brothers expressing genuine regret over the slavery sale that occurred 20 years earlier: *"We are verily (very) guilty concerning our brother (Joseph)"* Gen. 42:21.

The brothers were placed under great conviction when Joseph revealed his identity. Gen. 45:3 tells us that *the brothers were so scared (troubled) they couldn't even speak.* Can you imagine the startling fright when Joseph's brothers realized that the baby brother they had treated so horribly was in a position to determine if they lived or died?

A stunning conversion takes place when Joseph forgives his brothers. They didn't deserve forgiveness, but despite all the things they put him through, Joseph still loved his family. Joseph was more concerned about the well being of his father than he was about seeking revenge against his transgressors. In a further display of devotion, Joseph offers to care for his brother's belongings while they travel back home to retrieve their father.

Aren't fathers great? We sure don't deserve forgiveness for lots of things we do, but our Heavenly Father is faithful to forgive us when we ask. First

John 1:9 informs us, "*If we confess our sins, He is faithful and just to forgive us our sins, and to cleanse us from all unrighteousness.*" My partner sure didn't deserve forgiveness, let alone assistance, for the way he treated Mr. Johnboat on that tournament day, but he received it.

Forgiveness or not, it is important to be nice and display Christian behavior toward everyone. Besides, it pays not to step on the little guy for you never know when you might be totally dependent on him.

To order additional copies of

Heart Shot

Have your credit card ready and call:

1-877-421-READ (7323)

or please visit our web site at
www.pleasantword.com

Also available at:
www.amazon.com
and
www.barnesandnoble.com

Printed in the United States
25706LVS00001BA/103-186

9 781414 101934